KEY FACTS

COMPANY LAW

4th edition

Ann Ridley

ER
ON
E UK COMPANY

D0238234

Orders: please contact Bookpoint Ltd, 130 Milton Park, Abingdon, Oxon OX14 4SB.
Telephone: (44) 01235 827720. Fax: (44) 01235 400454. Lines are open from 9.00–5.00, Monday
to Saturday, with a 24-hour message answering service. You can also order through
our website www.hoddereducation.co.uk

British Library Cataloguing in Publication Data
A catalogue record for this title is available from The British Library.

ISBN 978 1 444 12284 8

First published 2002
Second Edition 2007
Third Edition 2009
This Edition 2011
Impression number   10 9 8 7 6 5 4 3 2 1
Year   2014 2013 2012 2011

Hachette UK's policy is to use papers that are natural, renewable and recyclable products and
made from wood grown in sustainable forests. The logging and manufacturing processes are
expected to conform to the environmental regulations of the country of origin.

Typeset by Transet Limited, Coventry, Warwickshire.
Printed in Great Britain for Hodder Education, an Hachette UK Company, 338 Euston Road,
London NW1 3BH by Cox & Wyman Ltd, Reading, Berks.

Contents

Preface

The Key Facts series is a practical and complete revision aid that can be used by students of law courses at all levels from A-Level to degree and in professional and vocational courses. The Key Facts series is designed to give a clear view of each subject. Most chapters open with an outline in diagram form of the points covered in that chapter. The points are then developed in a structured list form to make learning easier. Supporting cases are given throughout by name and, for some complex areas, facts are given to reinforce the point being made. The Key Facts series aims to accommodate the syllabus content on most qualifications in a subject area.

Company law may be a module of both law and business studies degree courses. It is also a vital subject in many professional and vocational courses. The detail and complexities of the subject can make it difficult for the student. The primary purpose of this book is as a revision aid and it is intended for use in conjunction with other, more substantive text books.

The Companies Act 2006 received the Royal Assent on 8 November 2006. This is a major piece of legislation, running to some 1,300 sections, and is the result of the Company Law Review which set out to modernise and simplify company law. Almost all sections of the Act are in force, following the final commencement date of 1 October 2009. For full details of commencement see the Department for Business, Innovations and Skills (BIS) website. In this book the Companies Act 2006 is treated as if fully in force.

The law is as I believe it to be on 1st January 2011.

1

Sources of company law

This chapter provides a brief summary of the main sources of company law: legislation, case law and European law. The Companies Act 2006 is the result of the most comprehensive review of company law ever undertaken and is the principal Act covering core company law. For useful information see the Department for Business, Innovation and Skills (BIS) website.

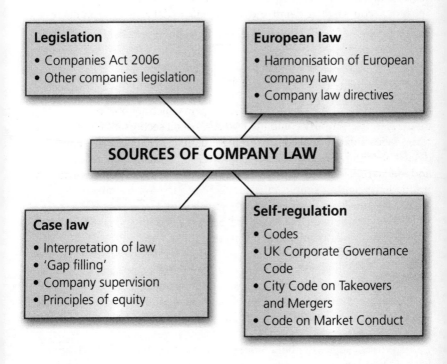

Legislation
- Companies Act 2006
- Other companies legislation

European law
- Harmonisation of European company law
- Company law directives

SOURCES OF COMPANY LAW

Case law
- Interpretation of law
- 'Gap filling'
- Company supervision
- Principles of equity

Self-regulation
- Codes
- UK Corporate Governance Code
- City Code on Takeovers and Mergers
- Code on Market Conduct

1.1 Legislation

1.1.1 Historical perspective

1. Legislation is the principal source of company law.
   - The first Act to allow incorporation was the Joint Stock Companies Act 1844.
   - The Joint Stock Companies Act 1856, sometimes called the 'first modern companies act', revised the system for setting up a company and this Act was the basis for the development of subsequent companies legislation.
   - There followed a long period of acts reforming the law, then a consolidating new Act.
   - Between 1948 and 1985 a number of statutes were passed to amend and add to the law and all of these were consolidated in the Companies Act 1985.
   - The 1989 Companies Act significantly amended the 1985 Act.

2. The Company Law Review was launched in 1998 and was the most comprehensive review of company law ever undertaken.

3. The Terms of Reference of the Company Law Review Steering Group (CLRSG), as set out in *Modern Company Law for a Competitive Economy: The Strategic Framework* (DTI 1999), were:
   ' (i) To consider how core company law can be modernised in order to provide a simple, efficient and cost-effective framework for carrying out business activity which:
      - (a) permits the maximum amount of freedom and flexibility to those organising and directing the enterprise;
      - (b) at the same time protects, through regulation where necessary, the interests of those involved with the enterprise, including shareholders, creditors and employees; and
      - (c) is drafted in clear, concise and unambiguous language which can be readily understood by those involved in business enterprise.
   (ii) To consider whether company law, partnership laws, and other legislation which establishes a legal form of business activity together provide an adequate choice of legal vehicle for business at all levels.
   (iii) To consider the proper relationship between company law and non-statutory standards of corporate behaviour.

(iv) To review the extent to which foreign companies operating in Great Britain should be regulated under British company law.

(v) To make recommendations accordingly.'

4. Wide consultation followed and the CLRSG produced four main documents under the general title *Modern Company Law for a Competitive Economy*. A large number of other reports and consultation papers were produced by the Law Commission, the Department of Trade and Industry (DTI) and the Company Law Review Steering Group itself. There followed two White Papers published in 2002 (*Modernising Company Law*) and 2005 (*The Company Law Reform Bill*). The latter included a draft Bill which, following further consultation and amendment, was introduced to the House of Lords on 1 November 2005.

5. The Companies Act 2006 received the Royal Assent on 8 November 2006. It repealed most of the Companies Act 1985, the Companies Act 1989 (which amended the 1985 Act) and the Business Names Act 1985.

1.1.2 Companies Act 2006

1. The Company Law Review set out to modernise and reform company law. The extent to which this has been achieved will be revealed over time as the Companies Act 2006 (CA 2006) is interpreted by the courts.

2. The Review aimed to facilitate enterprise by providing a framework of legislation that is clear and accessible, particularly with respect to small companies.

3. The idea of having a separate act for small closely-held companies was dropped early in the consultation and the 2006 Act, like the Companies Act 1985, covers all companies with exceptional provisions for private companies.

4. Corporate governance was a major theme of the Company Law Review, which can be seen in the provisions relating to meetings, shareholder engagement and directors' duties. The codification of directors' duties in Part 10 of the Act was much criticised in the course of consultation as being likely to lead to confusion rather than clarity. In this book, meetings and resolutions are considered in chapter 6, chapter 10 deals with principles of corporate governance, and sections 171–177 CA 2006 relating to directors' duties are described in chapter 12.

5. Ironically, the use of 'plain English' throughout the Act has also been criticised for its potential to bring new uncertainty to complex areas of law which are better described in terms that have acquired particular legal meaning as a result of interpretation by the courts and long-held usage by lawyers.

6. The Act has been implemented in stages over the period from Royal Assent in November 2006 to 1 October 2009. It is now substantially in force and has made significant changes to company law. Cases on the 2006 Act are beginning to come before the courts. Whether the aims of the reforms have been achieved will be seen as the provisions are applied and interpreted in the course of judicial decision-making.

1.1.3 Other companies legislation

1. As well as the CA 2006, the following Acts are important in the study of company law:
   - Criminal Justice Act 1993, which covers insider dealing (see chapter 13);
   - Insolvency Act 1986 (chapter 16);
   - Company Directors Disqualification Act 1986;
   - Financial Services and Markets Act 2000 (chapter 7 (offering shares to the public) and chapter 13 (market abuse));
   - Limited Liability Partnerships Act 2000;
   - Enterprise Act 2002 (chapter 16);
   - Corporate Manslaughter and Corporate Homicide Act 2007 (chapter 3).

2. A large number of orders, regulations and other statutory instruments also contribute to the body of company law.

1.2 Harmonisation of European company law

1. The harmonisation of company law, provided for in the Treaty of Rome (Art 44), has had a far-reaching impact on domestic company law and has resulted in a number of changes to the law.

2. The harmonisation programme has been carried out through a number of directives, which member states must enact into domestic law. Most are implemented by Acts of Parliament and are now contained in the

CA 2006. There have been 14 directives so far, of which the fifth, ninth and fourteenth have been withdrawn.

3. Changes introduced into English company law by the European harmonisation programme include:
   - First company law directive: the validity of company transactions and the eventual abolition of the *ultra vires* doctrine described in chapter 5;
   - Second: the raising and maintenance of capital (chapters 7 and 8);
   - Third: mergers of public companies by transfer of assets;
   - Fourth, seventh and eighth: set out requirements for company accounts and audit;
   - Sixth: demergers of public companies;
   - Tenth: cross-border mergers;
   - Eleventh: branches of certain kinds of company;
   - Twelfth: requires member states to allow single member private limited companies;
   - Thirteenth: company takeovers (chapter 15).

1.3 Case law

1. The importance of the influence of the courts in the development of company law is seen in a number of ways:
   - interpretation of the law;
   - gap filling – where the legislation did not cover a particular point, particularly in the early development of the law, principles were established by the courts;
   - company supervision – the courts have an extensive supervisory role and the conduct of companies is frequently reviewed by the courts, for example, a public company must seek the authority of the court if it wishes to reduce its capital (see chapter 8);
   - an understanding of company law requires knowledge of other areas of law where the law has been developed through judicial precedent, for example the law of agency mentioned in chapter 5;
   - principles of equity, developed through cases heard by the Court of Chancery initially, are an important element of company law. Examples include the fiduciary duties owed by directors to their companies (chapter 12) and winding up on the just and equitable ground under s 122(i)(g) Insolvency Act 1985 (chapter 14).

2. Section 170(4) CA 2006 provides that existing case law will be taken into account in the application and interpretation of the general duties of directors, set out in sections 171 to 177 of the 2006 Act.

1.4 Codes

1. In addition to legislation and case law, self-regulatory codes play a part and will need to be considered when studying certain aspects of company law. The City Code on Takeovers and Mergers was the most important example until it was given statutory authority in May 2006 (now Part 28 CA 2006). This is discussed in chapter 15.

2. The UK Corporate Governance Code, which imposes an obligation on public companies to comply with the Code or explain why they have not done so, is considered in chapter 10. The Code on Market Conduct developed by the Financial Services Authority under the Financial Services and Markets Act 2000 seeks to limit market abuse and market manipulation (chapter 13).

2

Company formation

Types of company:
- Limited by shares
- Limited by guarantee
- Unlimited
- Distinctions between public and private companies
- Community Interest companies
- European companies

Registration:
- Application and supporting documentation
- Role of the Registrar
- Certificate of incorporation – the company's 'birth certificate'

INCORPORATION AND PROMOTERS

Promoters:
- No statutory definition
- Described as 'One who undertakes to form a company ... and set it going'

Pre-incorporation contracts:
- Common law: *Kelner v Baxter* (1866); *Newborne v Sensolid* (1954)
- Art 7 First Company Law Directive
- s 51(1) Companies Act 2006
- Interpretation: *Phonogram v Lane* (1982)
- *Braymist Ltd v Wise Finance Ltd* (2001)
- *Hellmuth, Obata & Kassbaum Inc v Geoffrey King* (2000)
- *Oshkosh B'Gosh Inc v Dan Marble Inc Ltd* (1989)

2.1 Types of company

1. A company may be created by registration of documents with the Registrar of Companies under the Companies Act (currently CA 2006), registration with another public official or body under another act (e.g. under the Charities Act 1993), by statute or by Royal Charter. We are concerned only with the first method, that is, with 'registered companies'.

2. Companies may be registered as follows:
   - Limited by shares. This is a company with a share capital divided into shares which are issued to members. The liability of members on a winding up is limited to any amount unpaid on the shares.
   - Limited by guarantee. Section 3(3) CA 2006 provides that in such a company the liability of members is limited to the amount they agree to contribute in the event of the company being wound up. Prior to the CA 1980, a company could be limited by guarantee with a share capital. However, although a few such companies still exist, this is no longer possible.
   - Unlimited. A private company may be registered with unlimited liability, in which case the members will be liable to contribute to the whole of the company's debts on liquidation. Such companies are not subject to the disclosure requirements with respect to their accounts that apply to limited companies.

3. A major distinction is between public and private companies.
   - A public company is defined in s 4(2) CA 2006 as a company limited by shares (or by guarantee having a share capital) whose certificate of incorporation states that it is a public company in relation to which the requirements of the Act (or former Companies Acts) have been complied with.
   - A public company must have a minimum share capital, currently £50,000, of which 25% must be paid up.
   - Under s 4(1) a private company is defined as any company that is not a public company.
   - Both types of company may now be formed with one member: s 7(1) CA 2006).

4. A public company is subject to more stringent rules than a private company, especially in relation to disclosure, and throughout this book reference will be made to differences between public and private companies.

Public companies	Private companies
Defined by s 4(2) CA 2006	Defined by s 4(1) CA 2006
Limited by shares or by guarantee having a share capital	May be limited by shares or by guarantee, or unlimited
Minimum share capital requirements s 761	No minimum share capital requirement
Designated by 'plc' or Welsh equivalent	If limited, must include 'Limited' or 'Ltd' after name
Shares may be offered to the public	Shares may not be offered to the public

5. Community interest companies (CICs) were initially created by the Companies (Audit Investigations and Community Enterprise) Act 2004 for people who wanted to create social enterprises. The community interest company is recognised in s 6 CA 2006. The objects of such a company must show the intention to benefit the community and the directors must produce an annual report to show what the company has done for the benefit of the community. CICs do not have charitable status, but do enjoy lighter regulation than other companies.

6. European Companies: Regulation (EC) No 2157/2001 made it possible, from October 2004, to create a European public limited company, or *Societas Europaea*, where there is co-operation between at least two different companies in different member states.

7. The Limited Liability Partnership Act 2000 allows for incorporation by registration of a limited liability partnership (LLP). An LLP is a corporate body with a separate legal personality, while the relationship between the partners is the same as in a partnership. An LLP may only be formed for 'carrying on a lawful business with a view to profit'. Whereas an LLP must be for profit, a company can be registered for non-business purposes.

2.2 Registration

2.2.1 Documentation under the Companies Act 2006

1. To incorporate a company it is necessary to deliver an application together with the necessary documents to the Registrar of Companies for England and Wales or, for a company to be registered in Scotland, the Registrar of Companies for Scotland (s 9 CA 2006).
   - Since 2001 electronic incorporation has been possible for certain users, mainly company formation agents.
   - From January 2007 an online incorporation facility is available for individual users as well.

2. The application must contain the following information:
   - the company's proposed name;
   - the part of the United Kingdom where it is to be registered – whether in England and Wales, Scotland or Northern Ireland;
   - whether the members are to have limited liability and, if so, whether by share or guarantee;
   - whether the company is to be a public or private company.

3. The application must be accompanied by supporting documents:
   (a) The memorandum of association, which must include a statement that the subscribers wish to form a company and, in the case of a company with a share capital, that they agree to take at least one share each. One subscriber can form a company and there is no upper limit.
   (b) The company's constitution, that is the articles of association, which may be in the form of the appropriate model articles unless excluded or modified to suit the needs of the particular company.
   (c) A statement of capital and the initial shareholdings. This gives details of the shares that the company will issue when it is incorporated and to whom they will be issued. The statement must be updated each time new shares are issued.
   (d) A statement of the company's proposed officers, setting out details of the proposed director(s) and secretary (if applicable), together with a consent by each person to act in the proposed role. A private company may have only one director, a public company must have at least two (s 154 CA 2006). Those named will take up office on the date of incorporation.

(e) A statement of compliance, which states that the registration requirements set out in the Companies Act 2006 have been complied with.

4. The prescribed fee must be paid.

5. With respect to the articles note the following:
   - Companies registered under the Companies Act 1985 may have articles in the form of Table A, CA 1985, which were the same for public and private companies. See chapter 4 for more detail.
   - The Companies Act 2006 model articles will apply to new companies incorporated on or after 1 October 2009. There are separate model articles for public companies limited by shares, companies limited by guarantee and private companies limited by shares.
   - Under CA 2006 the articles of association comprise the main constitutional document.

6. One person can form any kind of company, including a public company: s 7(1) CA 2006. Under CA 1985 a public company had to have at least two members.

2.2.2 Registrar's role

1. If all the documentation is in order, the Registrar issues a certificate of incorporation, which is conclusive evidence:
   - that the requirements of the Act in respect of registration and of matters precedent and incidental to it have been complied with, and that the association is a company authorised to be registered, and is duly registered under the Act; and
   - that if the certificate contains a statement that the company is a public company, it is in fact such a company.

2. Public notice must be given that the memorandum and articles of association have been received by Companies House.

3. Section 7(2) CA 2006 provides that a company may not be formed for an unlawful purpose. The Registrar may refuse registration if he considers this to be the case.

4. Under previous companies legislation, every company's memorandum of association contained an objects clause which, in theory, set out the purpose for which the company was being set up. This allowed the Registrar, in certain cases, to determine that the purpose was unlawful:

R v Registrar of Companies, ex parte Bowen (1914); *R v Registrar of Companies, ex parte AG* (1980) reported (1991).

5. Under the CA 2006 a company is not required to have an objects clause (see chapter 5).

6. If the Registrar is satisfied that the requirements of the Act have been complied with, he must register the company (s 14 CA 2006). A company comes into existence on the date stated on the certificate of incorporation.

7. A refusal by the Registrar to register a company is subject to judicial review.

8. A public company cannot start trading until a trading certificate has been issued under s 761 CA 2006, whereas a private company can trade immediately on incorporation.

2.2.3 Off the shelf companies

It is also possible to buy a company 'off the shelf'. Such companies are incorporated by registration agents and are available for purchase relatively cheaply. When the ready-made company is sold, its shares are transferred to nominees of the purchaser. The original directors and secretary resign and new directors and secretary are appointed by the purchaser.

2.2.4 Company names

1. The CA 2006, and associated statutory instruments, contain a number of provisions relating to company names, including:
   - the name of a private company limited by shares must end with 'ltd' or 'limited', or in the case of company registered in Wales, the Welsh equivalent;
   - a public company's name must end with 'public limited company', 'plc' or the Welsh equivalent;
   - a company may not be registered with a name which is illegal or which the Registrar considers to be offensive or misleading;
   - permission is needed to use certain words, for example anything that suggests that the company is connected with government or a local authority;
   - under s 66 CA 2006 a company may not register a name that is the same or too like one already registered on the Registrar's index

of names. There are exceptions to this and ss 67 and 68 contain provisions dealing with situations where such names are registered in error.

2. If a company's name is deceptively similar to that of another business to the extent that damage may be caused to the reputation or goodwill of the other business, an action in the tort of passing off may provide a remedy.

2.3 Promoters

2.3.1 Introduction

1. During the nineteenth century it was common for people setting up a new company to raise money by offering shares to the public. This provided an opportunity for abuse and the principles described below were developed in response to this.

2. As a result of legal regulation and the Stock Exchange Listing Rules, the law relating to duties of promoters is now of little practical importance as far as public companies are concerned. It may still have some relevance to private companies.

2.3.2 Who is a promoter?

1. The term *promoter* is one of fact, not of law. A promoter has been described as: 'One who undertakes to form a company with reference to a given project and to set it going, and who takes the necessary steps to accomplish that purpose' (Cockburn CJ, *Twycross v Grant* (1877)).

2. People who act in a purely administrative capacity (e.g. solicitors and accountants) do not become promoters simply by carrying out a professional service.

3. Promoters working together to set up a company are not necessarily partners (*Keith Spicer v Mansell* (1970)).

4. In each case the courts will look to the surrounding facts to establish whether a person is a promoter.

2.3.3 Duties of a promoter

1. As the early cases show, there is often the opportunity for a promoter to abuse his position and take a profit from deals made in the course of

promotion. For example, they may purchase property which they later sell to the company: *Erlanger v New Sombrero Phosphate Co* (1878).

2. In equity a promoter owes a fiduciary duty to the company when it is incorporated. The fiduciary relationship begins as soon as the promoter starts to take steps to set up the company.

3. The essence of this duty is in 'good faith, fair dealing and full disclosure'. The most important aspect of the duty is that the promoter may not make a secret profit and must declare an interest or profit in any transaction that involves the company.

4. Some problems arise as to how and to whom disclosure should be made. Disclosure to, and approval by, a board of directors who are independent of the promoters is sufficient, as is disclosure in a prospectus inviting prospective shareholders to invest in the company. Disclosure to the members as a whole has long been recognised as effective (*Erlanger v New Sombrero Phosphate Co* (1878); *Lagunas Nitrate Co v Lagunas Syndicate* (1899)).

5. Partial disclosure is insufficient – promoters must declare the whole profit: *Gluckstein v Barnes* (1900).

6. Remedies of the company for breach of fiduciary duty include:
   - rescission of any contract entered into as a result of non-disclosure or misrepresentation;
   - recovery of any secret profit;
   - imposition of a constructive trust;
   - damages for breach of fiduciary duty (*Re Leeds & Hanley Theatres* (1902)) – however, the scope of this remedy is somewhat uncertain;
   - damages for deceit.

7. At common law a promoter may be liable in tort for loss caused by fraud or negligence.

2.4 Pre-incorporation contracts

1. The company, once incorporated, is recognised by the law as a separate legal person. As such it can act only through agents (see chapter 5). Agency problems arise when a person purports to make a contract for a company prior to incorporation because the principal (the company) does not yet exist.

2. A contract made on behalf of a company before its incorporation does not bind the company, nor can it be enforced or ratified by the company after incorporation. However, there may be a remedy against the person purportedly acting for the company.

3. Early cases distinguished between contracts made 'for and on behalf of' the company (*Kelner v Baxter* (1866), where it was held that the person who purported to act as agent was personally liable in place of the non-existent principal), and those where the promoter signed his own name to authenticate the name of the company (*Newborne v Sensolid* (1954), where it was held that because the company did not exist there was no contract). The fine distinctions suggested by these and other cases made the position at common law quite complex. This has, however, been superseded by statute.

4. Article 7 of the First Company Law Directive provides: 'If, before a company being formed has acquired legal personality, action has been carried out in its name and the company does not assume the obligations arising from such action, the persons who acted shall, without limit, be jointly and severally liable therefore unless otherwise agreed'.

5. This was implemented by the European Communities Act 1972 and is now re-enacted as s 51(1) CA 2006 which provides: 'A contract that purports to be made by or on behalf of a company at a time when the company has not been formed has effect, subject to any agreement to the contrary, as one made with the person purporting to act for the company or as agent for it, and he is personally liable on the contract accordingly'.

6. The section was interpreted in *Phonogram v Lane* (1982) in which it was held:
    - in applying this section the subtle distinctions developed by the courts will not be made;
    - the section applies whether the process of incorporation has been started or not (i.e. it is not necessary for the company to be in the course of being formed);
    - the section applies whether or not the company is eventually incorporated;
    - it applies to a contract purportedly made on behalf of a company intended to be incorporated outside Great Britain as long as the contract is governed by the law of England and Wales or of Scotland: *Hellmuth, Obata & Kassbaum Inc v Geoffrey King* (2000).

7. Section 51(1) CA 2006 makes it clear that a purported agent will be liable under a pre-incorporation contract (unless the parties have agreed otherwise).

8. Until recently it was unclear whether an agent would be able to enforce such a contract. This issue was addressed in *Braymist Ltd v Wise Finance Ltd* (2001) and it was held that where s 51(1) applies, a fully effective contract is deemed to have been concluded between the purported agent and the contracting party, conferring both liability and a right of action on the purported agent.

9. Section 51(2) CA 2006 provides that the same provisions apply to a deed.

10. A pre-incorporation contract cannot be ratified by the company after incorporation. The company did not exist when the contract was purportedly made on its behalf and the purported agent cannot retro-spectively be given authority to act on behalf of a non-existent entity. The only way that the company can assume liability on the contract is by way of novation – that is by entering into a new contract with the contractor.

11. The section has limitations:
    (a) it will not apply when a company has been bought off the shelf and is in the process of changing its name. In this situation the company does not comply with the requirement in s 51(1) that it 'has not been formed' (*Oshkosh B'Gosh Inc v Dan Marbel Inc Ltd* (1989));
    (b) the agent must purport to make the contract on behalf of a new company, so the section will not apply in a situation where the parties are unaware that the company has been dissolved (*Cotronic (UK) Ltd v Dezonie* (1991)).

3

Corporate personality

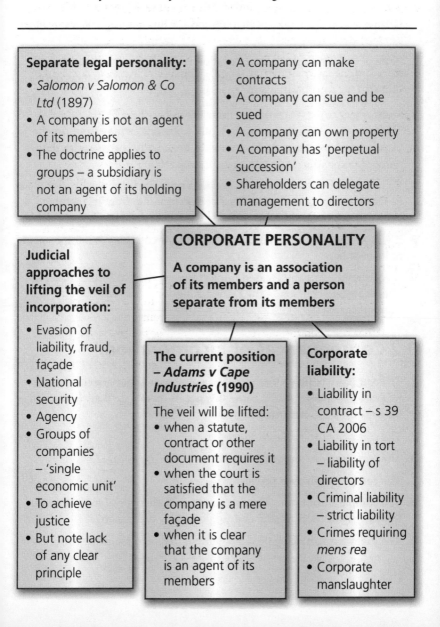

Separate legal personality:

- *Salomon v Salomon & Co Ltd* (1897)
- A company is not an agent of its members
- The doctrine applies to groups – a subsidiary is not an agent of its holding company

- A company can make contracts
- A company can sue and be sued
- A company can own property
- A company has 'perpetual succession'
- Shareholders can delegate management to directors

CORPORATE PERSONALITY

A company is an association of its members and a person separate from its members

Judicial approaches to lifting the veil of incorporation:

- Evasion of liability, fraud, façade
- National security
- Agency
- Groups of companies – 'single economic unit'
- To achieve justice
- But note lack of any clear principle

The current position – *Adams v Cape Industries* (1990)

The veil will be lifted:
- when a statute, contract or other document requires it
- when the court is satisfied that the company is a mere façade
- when it is clear that the company is an agent of its members

Corporate liability:

- Liability in contract – s 39 CA 2006
- Liability in tort – liability of directors
- Criminal liability – strict liability
- Crimes requiring *mens rea*
- Corporate manslaughter

3.1 Introduction

1. A company is both a separate legal person and an association of its members. This is an underpinning feature of company law. This chapter will describe the principles and the limitations of separate legal personality.

2. Issue of the certificate of incorporation is conclusive evidence that all the requirements of the Companies Act 2006 in relation to incorporation have been complied with (s 15(4) CA 2006).

3. Section 16(2) CA 2006 provides that 'The subscribers to the memorandum, together with such other persons as may from time to time become members of the company, are a body corporate by the name stated in the certificate of incorporation'.

4. By incorporation, the company acquires separate legal personality; that is, the company is recognised as a person separate from its members, a principle established in *Salomon v Salomon & Co Ltd* (1897).

5. It was further established in this case that the company is not the agent of its members.

6. A registered company created under foreign law is also recognised as a separate legal person in the United Kingdom (*Arab Monetary Fund v Hashim (No 3)* (1991)).

3.2 Consequences of incorporation

1. The company is an association of its members and a person separate from its members. It is the company, not its members, that conducts the business of the company.

2. The company can make contracts.

3. The company can sue and be sued.

4. The company can own property.

5. The company continues in existence despite changes of membership. In other words, a company enjoys 'perpetual succession'.

6. The members can delegate management to directors.

3.3 The *Salomon* principle

1. The principle of separate legal personality is a powerful device, allowing incorporators to manage commercial risk, but in certain situations it can be used unfairly or fraudulently.

2. The concept of separate personality also extends to groups of companies, with each subsidiary in a group having a separate identity.

3. Furthermore, as a company is not an agent of its members, it follows that, unless there is specific evidence of an agency arrangement, a subsidiary is not an agent of its parent company (see further at section 3.4.2).

4. The following cases are examples of affirmation of the *Salomon* principle by the courts.

   - *Macaura v Northern Assurance* (1925): a shareholder had no insurable interest in property owned by the company. Note that in this case the principle was applied to the disadvantage of the shareholder.
   - *Lee v Lee's Air Farming* (1961): a company can employ one of its members who will have all statutory and other rights against the company.
   - *Secretary of State for Trade and Industry v Bottrill* (1999): a sole shareholder can be employed by the company and will have rights under the Employment Rights Act 1996.
   - *Secretary of State for Business, Enterprise and Regulatory Reform v Neurfeld* (2009): the Court of Appeal reviewed the law and held that a director of a company can be an employee as long as he is employed under a genuine contract of employment and not a contract for services.
   - *R v Philippou* (1989): the sole directors and shareholders withdrew funds from the company's account in London and bought themselves a property in Spain. The company went into liquidation leaving very large debts. They were charged with stealing from the company and argued that as they were the only directors, the withdrawal had the consent of the company. The Court of Appeal refused to accept this argument.
   - *Foss v Harbottle* (1843): since a company is a legal person separate from its members, a member cannot bring an action to redress a wrong done to the company, but note the statutory provisions in Part 11 CA 2006 considered in chapter 14.

3.4 Lifting the corporate veil

1. The notion that a company is recognised as a person separate from its members is often described as the 'veil of incorporation'.

2. In certain circumstances the veil of incorporation has been lifted to avoid the consequences of separate legal personality. Furthermore, there are a number of statutory exceptions to the principle.

3. Limited liability is not a direct consequence of the corporate entity principle (it is possible to form an unlimited company), but the vast majority of companies are limited and the concept goes hand-in-hand with the principle of separate personality. If the veil is lifted this right to limited liability may be lost.

4. The courts have been very reluctant to lift the veil in order to impose personal liability for the company's debts on a shareholder or director.

5. Note that in groups of companies each company has the benefit of separate legal personality, but there are a number of statutory exceptions in relation to group accounts.

3.4.1 Judicial approaches

In certain circumstances, the *Salomon* principle can be used in ways that appear to be unjust to third parties, creditors or even the shareholders themselves. The development of the law shows how the courts have sometimes taken the view that the veil of incorporation should be lifted to avoid abuse of separate personality. The approach has not always been consistent and it is difficult to identify clear principles to determine when the courts may be prepared to lift the veil and when they would decline to do so.

1. The Companies Act 2006 itself contains provisions that have the effect of lifting the veil in certain circumstances (see section 3.4.3) and the courts have also interpreted provisions in other statutes so as to require that the veil should be lifted. However, in *Dimbleby & Sons Ltd v National Union of Journalists* (1984) it was held that any parliamentary intention that the veil should be lifted must be expressed in 'clear and unambiguous language'.

2. The courts have lifted the veil in cases involving national security, particularly in times of war.

3. The veil has been lifted in cases where it has been shown that the corporate form was being used as a façade in order to avoid liability or to gain an illegitimate benefit for the shareholders. Examples include:

   (a) evasion of liability to pay tax (*Commissioners of Inland Revenue v Land Securities Investment Trust Ltd* (1969); *Littlewoods Mail Order Stores Ltd v Inland Revenue Commissioners* (1969));

   (b) evasion of a restraint of trade clause in a contract of employment (*Gilford Motor Co Ltd v Horne* (1933); *Dadourian Group International Inc v Simms* (2006));

   (c) attempt to avoid an order of specific performance (*Jones v Lipman* (1962)).

4. In the cases above, those in control of the company used the corporate form to commit a wrong. The veil will not be lifted when the company is controlled by others who have had no part in the wrongdoing (*Hashem v Shayif* (2008)) or where there has been no impropriety or attempt to hide the facts (*Ord v Belhaven Pubs Ltd* (1998)).

3.4.2 Groups

A number of cases have involved groups of companies and several different approaches have been employed by the courts.

1. **Agency**: it was held in *Salomon v Salomon* (1895) that a company is not an agent of its shareholders. However, the agency argument has been used in a number of cases involving groups of companies. Every company in a group is recognised as a separate legal person and it has been argued that a subsidiary is in certain circumstances an agent of the holding company. If on the facts of the case there is actual evidence of an agency existing, this is consistent with the principle of separate legal personality, but the issue is usually whether an agency can be inferred.

   (a) In *FG Films Ltd* (1953) the court inferred agency in a case where a United Kingdom company was set up in order to acquire film distribution rights in the United Kingdom for an American holding company.

   (b) In *Smith, Stone & Knight Ltd v Birmingham Corporation* (1939) the court laid down guidelines to establish whether an agency could be implied between a holding company and its subsidiaries. However, this case has been criticised and has not been followed.

   (c) In *JH Rayner (Mincing Lane) Ltd v Department of Trade and Industry* (1989) it was held that an agency cannot be inferred from the mere fact that the company is controlled by its shareholders.

2. **Single economic unit:** the high water mark of the courts' willingness to lift veils was *DHN Food Distributors Ltd v Tower Hamlets LBC* (1975), in which it was held that a group of companies was a single economic unit, thus enabling the group to claim compensation on the compulsory purchase of land even though the land from which the business operated was owned by a subsidiary and the business was operated by the parent company.

3. This case was disapproved by the House of Lords in *Woolfson v Strathclyde Regional Council* (1978) and the argument was not accepted in subsequent cases, including *Re Southard & Co Ltd* (1979) and *Adams v Cape Industries* (1990).

4. **Justice:** in some cases the courts have been willing to accept that the veil can be lifted where this is necessary in order to achieve justice, for example *Creasey v Breachwood Motors Ltd* (1992). However, this view has not been accepted in recent cases, and *Creasey* was overruled by the Court of Appeal in *Ord v Belhaven Pubs Ltd* (1998).

5. In the important case of *Adams v Cape Industries* (1990) the Court of Appeal reviewed the arguments for lifting the veil discussed above, in particular the agency argument, the single economic unit argument and the 'façade' argument, and held that none of these applied on the facts.

6. The case signalled a shift towards the view that in the absence of fraud, incorporators can rely on the principle of separate corporate personality. This view has been affirmed in *Ord v Belhaven Pubs Ltd* (1998), where it was held that the court may not lift the veil in situations where there is no attempt to hide the true facts, no ulterior motive and no impropriety.

7. On the other hand where impropriety can be shown the façade argument may be accepted so that the court is willing to lift the veil, as in *Trustor AB v Smallbone (No 2)* (2001) where a company was used as a device for the receipt of misappropriated funds. In circumstances where a company may be seen as a 'sham' or an abuse of the corporate form so as to evade liability or gain an unjust benefit, the veil may be lifted. The motive behind the establishment of a company may be relevant, for example if it was used as a device to conceal the true facts and to avoid limitations on a shareholder's conduct (as in *Gilford Motors v Horne*) or to avoid pre-existing liabilities.

8. The current situation can be summarised as follows:
   (a) Although agency cannot usually be inferred, effect will be given to an express agency agreement between a company and its members or between companies in a group. An express agency affirms the principle of separate personality.
   (b) Following *Adams v Cape Industries*, it seems that the only circumstances in which the courts are likely to lift the veil are now:
   - when the court is construing a statute, contract or other document which requires the veil to be lifted;
   - when the court is satisfied that the company is a 'mere façade', so that there is an abuse of the corporate form;
   - when it can be established that the company is an authorised agent of its controllers or its members, corporate or human.

9. However, each case is considered on its facts and there are suggestions in some recent cases that the Court of Appeal may be more willing than in Adams to treat a group of companies as a single concern: see *Beckett Investment Management Group Ltd v Hall* (2007).

3.4.3 Statutory exceptions

1. There are a number of statutory provisions in the Companies Act 2006 that have the effect of lifting the veil.

2. Section 767(3) CA 2006 provides that if a public company acts before obtaining a trading certificate, all the officers and directors are liable to fines and if the company fails to comply within 21 days the directors are liable to indemnify anyone who suffered loss as a result of the transaction.

3. For groups of companies, s 399 provides that, unless subject to the small companies regime or otherwise exempt, the directors of a parent company must file group accounts.

4. Other Acts also provide examples: ss 213 and 214 Insolvency Act 1986, which provide that in cases of fraudulent trading and wrongful trading a director may be liable to make a contribution to the company's assets, and s 15 Company Directors Disqualification Act 1986 which provides that a person involved in the management of a company in contravention of a disqualification order is liable for the debts of the company.

3.5 Corporate liability

The fact that a company is an artificial person raises interesting questions as to the limits of a company's liability for wrongful acts.

3.5.1 Liability in contract

1. A company is a legal person separate from its members. One of the most important consequences of incorporation is that a company can enter into contracts and other commercial transactions and is fully liable for the debts it incurs.

2. A company can only act through its agents and the usual principles of agency, together with the provisions in s 40 CA 2006, will be applied in deciding whether a company is liable on any contract (see further chapter 5). Note that the agent is not a party to the contract, so it is the company and not its agents that will be liable for breach of contract.

3. A company must act in accordance with its constitution. The CA 2006 s 31 provides that a company has unlimited capacity unless it chooses to restrict its capacity by inserting an objects clause, which may then limit its capacity to make certain contracts. Section 39 CA 2006 is designed to provide security of contract to persons dealing with a company and this is discussed further in chapter 5.

3.5.2 Liability in tort: vicarious liability

1. In tort, a company may be held vicariously liable for the wrongful acts of its officers and employees as long as they were acting in the course of their employment. The employee who commits the act will also be liable as the primary tortfeasor.

2. Vicarious liability has been described as 'a loss distribution device based on grounds of social and economic policy' (Lord Millett in *Dubai Aluminium Co Ltd v Salaam* (2002)). The company may be held liable for a tort of someone else, for example its employee or agent.

3.5.3 When are directors liable in tort?

1. If a director, acting for a company, causes the company to commit a tort it is the company not the director who becomes liable. However, if a director is acting in a personal capacity or assumes personal responsibility he or she will be liable for the tort. Difficult questions

arise as it is not always easy to establish whether the director has acted in a personal capacity and each case depends on its own facts: see *Fairline Shipping Corporation v Adamson* (1975); *Mancetter Developments Ltd v Garmanson Ltd* (1986); and *MCA Records Inc v Charly Records Ltd* (2003).

2. Similar issues arise in cases involving the tort of negligent misrepresentation if a director provides advice on behalf of the company. In *Williams v Natural Health Foods Ltd* (1998) advice was given by a company to the claimant. The advice, which had been produced by the managing director (who was also the main shareholder) and was acted upon by the claimant, turned out to be inaccurate. By the time the action was brought the company had ceased to exist and the question arose whether the managing director could be liable. The issue was whether this was a personal act of the director rather than one carried out for the business purposes of the company. It was held that the managing director had not assumed personal responsibility and was not liable.

3. If a director were held to be personally liable for the tort, this would effectively remove the protection of incorporation and, in the case of a limited company, of limited liability. In *Williams* Lord Steyn said: '[In] order to establish personal liability under the principle of Hedley Byrne [*Hedley Byrne v Heller* (1964)], which requires the existence of a special relationship between plaintiff and tortfeasor, it is not sufficient that there should have been a special relationship with the principal. There must have been an assumption of responsibility such as to create a special relationship with the director or employee himself'. In this case it had not been possible to show that such a relationship existed.

4. However, it may be possible to show that the director is personally liable for a tort involving fraud or dishonesty, as in *Standard Chartered Bank v Pakistan National Shipping Corp (Nos 2 and 4)* (2002 and 2003), where both the director and the company were sued for the tort of deceit. See also *Contex Drouzhba Ltd v Wiseman* (2007).

3.5.4 Liability for crime

1. Companies can commit crimes of strict liability and there are a large number of regulatory offences that apply to companies. In such cases it is necessary only to show that the company committed the criminal act (*actus reus*): *Alphacell Ltd v Woodward* (1972).

2. There are certain crimes which it is impossible for a company to commit since the *actus reus* could not be committed by an artificial person, for example driving a vehicle in an unsafe condition (*Richmond-on-Thames BC v Pinn & Wheeler Ltd* (1989)).

3. There are also obvious limitations on the sanctions that can be applied to companies: notably, a company cannot be imprisoned.

4. In recent years debate has centred on whether a company, being a legal entity without a mind of its own, is able to form the necessary *mens rea* for the offence in question.

5. In three cases in 1944 companies were convicted of offences requiring *mens rea* (*DPP v Kent & Sussex Contractors*; *R v ICR Haulage Ltd*; *Moore v Bresler*).

6. The principle that in certain circumstances a company can commit a crime requiring *mens rea* was recognised by the House of Lords in *Tesco Supermarkets Ltd v Nattrass* (1972).

3.5.5 Corporate manslaughter

1. Following the capsize of the Herald of Free Enterprise, the question of whether a company could be convicted of manslaughter was considered. In *R v P&O European Ferries (Dover) Ltd* (1990) it was held that it was possible for a company to commit manslaughter, as long as it could be established that a person who could be identified as the 'mind and will of the company' could be found guilty of the offence: this became known as the identification principle. In that case, however, the company was not guilty.

2. The first successful prosecution of a company for manslaughter was *R v Kite* (1996), in which the company was fined £60,000 on conviction. The managing director of the company was convicted and was sentenced to three years imprisonment, reduced by the Court of Appeal to two years. In this case, unlike *P&O European Ferries*, the managing director could be seen as the controlling 'mind and will' of the company and the company was therefore guilty of the offence.

3. Some of the difficulties are highlighted in *Attorney General's Reference (No 2 of 1999)* in which the trial judge directed the acquittal of Great Western Trains Ltd following a rail accident which caused the deaths of seven people. It had not been possible to prove gross negligence on the part of any individual who could be identified as the directing mind and will of the company.

4. In March 1996, the Law Commission published a report *Legislating the Criminal Code: Involuntary Manslaughter* (Law Com No 237), in which the Commission made a number of recommendations, including proposals for a new offence of corporate killing, separate from the offences that can be committed by individuals. After further consultation and long delays the Corporate Manslaughter and Corporate Homicide Act 2007 was passed in July 2007.

5. The Act abolishes the common law offence of corporate manslaughter by gross negligence (s 20) and signals a shift from the identification principle to the concept of management failure. Whereas previously it had been necessary to show that death had been caused by a person or persons who could be identified as the 'mind and will' of the company, the Act now focuses on the way an organisation is managed by its 'senior management'.

6. It provides that an organisation (it includes partnerships as well as corporations) will be guilty of manslaughter if the way in which its activities are managed or organised by senior management:
   - causes the death of a person or persons, and
   - amounts to a gross breach of the relevant duty of care owed by the organisation to the victim(s) (s 1(1)).
   - It is further provided that the way the company's activities are managed or organised must be a substantial element in the breach referred to above (s 1(3)).

7. Senior management is defined in s 1(4) of the Act as those who play a significant role in:
   - making decisions about how the whole, or a substantial part, of an organisation's activities are to be managed or organised, or
   - actually managing or organising the whole or a substantial part of those activities.

8. Section 2, read with ss 3–7, defines 'relevant duty of care', which is a question of law for the judge. A breach of duty is a 'gross breach' if the alleged conduct falls far below what can reasonably be expected of the organisation in the circumstances.

9. It is up to the jury to decide whether the death was caused by a gross breach of duty and s 8 sets out the factors that the jury must consider in coming to a decision.

10. On conviction an organisation is liable to pay a fine. The Act also gives power to the court to make:

- a remedial order, requiring the organisation to take steps to remedy the breach or any deficiency relating to health and safety (s 9), and
- a publicity order, requiring the organisation to publicise the fact that it has been convicted of the offence and other details as ordered by the court is provided for in s 10, but this has not been brought into force.

4

Articles of association

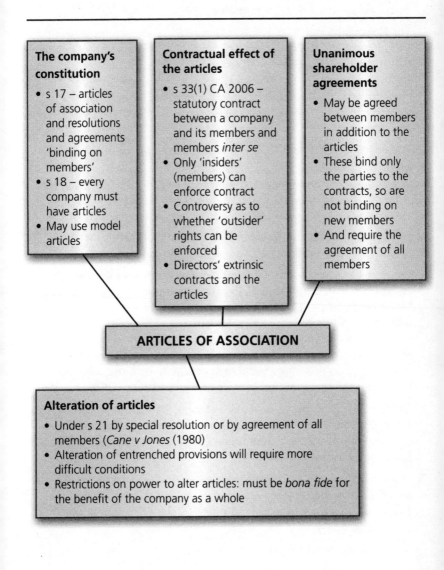

The company's constitution

- s 17 – articles of association and resolutions and agreements 'binding on members'
- s 18 – every company must have articles
- May use model articles

Contractual effect of the articles

- s 33(1) CA 2006 – statutory contract between a company and its members and members *inter se*
- Only 'insiders' (members) can enforce contract
- Controversy as to whether 'outsider' rights can be enforced
- Directors' extrinsic contracts and the articles

Unanimous shareholder agreements

- May be agreed between members in addition to the articles
- These bind only the parties to the contracts, so are not binding on new members
- And require the agreement of all members

ARTICLES OF ASSOCIATION

Alteration of articles

- Under s 21 by special resolution or by agreement of all members (*Cane v Jones* (1980)
- Alteration of entrenched provisions will require more difficult conditions
- Restrictions on power to alter articles: must be *bona fide* for the benefit of the company as a whole

4.1 The company's constitution

1. Under previous Companies Acts every company was required to have two important constitutional documents: a memorandum of association and articles of association.

2. The Companies Act 2006 (CA 2006) has reduced the significance of the memorandum, which now simply contains an undertaking by each of the subscribers that they intend to form a company and agree to take at least one share each. The articles are now the company's main constitutional document. Information previously set out in the memorandum of association is now given as part of the application for registration.

3. Under s 17 CA 2006 a company's constitutional documents include:
   - the company's articles, and
   - resolutions and agreements 'binding on members' which, in terms of s 29, includes any special resolution and a broad range of other resolutions and agreements.

4. Section 18 provides that every company must have articles which contain the rules on how the company is to be run.

5. Previous Companies Acts included model articles, for example Table A CA 1985, which applied to both private and public companies and which could be adopted with or without amendments. Companies registered under previous Acts may continue to have as their constitution what has been termed an 'old style memorandum' and articles which may be in the form of Table A. Companies registered under previous acts may amend their articles to conform with the CA 2006 if the company agrees to do so by special resolution.

6. The CA 2006 gives power to the Secretary of State for Business Innovation and Skills to prescribe separate model articles for public companies, private companies limited by shares and private companies limited by guarantee: s 19(2).

7. A company may adopt the relevant model articles in whole or in part, as was the case under previous legislation. Model articles have been published for private companies limited by shares and for public companies.

4.2 Contractual effect of the constitution

1. The ownership of shares in a company gives rise to certain rights and obligations. A company is an artificial person in its own right as well as an association of its members, and is therefore able to contract with its members.

2. Section 33(1) CA 2006 (previously s 14 CA 1985) provides: 'The provisions of a company's constitution bind the company and its members to the same extent as if there were covenants on the part of the company and of each member to observe those provisions'.

3. Previous versions of this provision referred only to 'covenants on the part of each member to observe all the provisions of the memorandum and the articles', making no mention of the company's obligation. Although it has been generally accepted that there is a contract between the company and its members (*Hickman v Kent or Romney Marsh Sheepbreeders Association* (1915)), the change of wording to 'covenants on the part of *the company and of* each member' removes any doubt.

4. Under previous legislation the equivalent section referred to the memorandum and articles, although discussion focused on the articles since this document contained the rules for internal management of the company. Section 33 CA 2006 refers to the constitution and although the principal constitutional document is the articles of association, this may also include certain resolutions (see s 17).

4.2.1 Special features of the s 33 contract

Ordinary contract	s 33 contract
Terms agreed by parties	Member usually accepts terms by purchase of shares in company
Terms provide for obligations/rights which when performed come to an end	The constitution creates ongoing rights/obligations – sometimes referred to as a relational contract
Terms may only be altered by agreement	Articles can be altered by special resolution (s 21 CA 2006)
Rectification available	Rectification not available (*Scott v Scott* (1940))

Damages are the usual remedy for breach	Damages usually not appropriate (but may be claimed for liquidated sum, e.g. dividend); a declaration is the usual remedy

1. The distinctions between an ordinary contract and the statutory contract were noted in *Bratton Seymour Service Co Ltd v Oxenborough* (1992). In this case the Court of Appeal refused to imply a term into the articles imposing a financial obligation on members in order to give the articles 'business efficacy'. The articles are a public document and it is important that third parties, especially prospective members, are able to rely on the accuracy of these documents as registered.

2. However, in *Folkes Group plc v Alexander* (2002) the court construed an article by adding five words to correct what, according to the evidence, must have been a drafting error. This case should be treated as exceptional, and the general principle remains that external factors should not be taken into account when construing articles of association.

4.2.2 The scope of the statutory contract

1. The scope of the s 33 contract has been considered in a number of cases, which cannot easily be reconciled. The following points are established:
   (a) Once registered, the articles constitute a contract between the members and the company and between the members *inter se* (*Wood v Odessa Waterworks Co* (1889)). This is now more clearly stated in the 2006 Act than in previous legislation. This contract gives rise to:
      ■ contractual rights between the company and its members (*Hickman v Kent or Romney Marsh Sheep-Breeders Association* (1915));
      ■ contractual rights for shareholders against fellow shareholders (*Rayfield v Hands* (1960)).
   (b) Only an '**insider**' (a member in this context), can enforce the contract and only those rights that are held in his or her capacity as a member fall within the scope of s 33.

(c) A claim under s 33 made by an **'outsider'** (that is, a person claiming in a capacity other than that of member) will not succeed (*Eley v Positive Government Security Life Assurance* (1876); *Beattie v E and F Beattie* (1938)). It should be noted here that 'outsider' has been strictly defined and a claim based on rights held as a director will fail, even if the director is also a member.

(d) A member's statutory rights cannot be limited by the articles, for example in *Baring-Gould v Sharpington Combined Pick & Shovel Syndicate* (1899) a resolution in the articles purporting to limit members' rights under what is now s 111(2) Insolvency Act 1986 could not be enforced.

4.2.3 What rights can be enforced?

1. The statutory contract confers on a member, in his capacity as a member, the right to bring a personal action to enforce certain constitutional rights. There are conflicting cases on what may be enforced under s 33: see for example *MacDougall v Gardiner* (1875) where the refusal by the chairman to accept a request for a poll in breach of the articles was held to be an internal irregularity which could be put right by the company's own mechanisms and therefore was not enforceable by personal action. Compare this with *Pender v Lushington* (1877) below.

2. The following rights contained in the articles have been enforced by members:
   - a provision in the articles requiring directors to purchase shares from a member wishing to leave the company (*Rayfield v Hands*);
   - a right to exercise a vote at a general meeting (*Pender v Lushington* (1877));
   - payment of a dividend, duly declared (*Wood v Odessa Waterworks Co*) – in this case a member was able to demand payment in cash as implied by the articles, even though the general meeting had agreed to payment by way of debenture;
   - a right to enforce a veto by directors on certain acts (*Salmon v Quin & Axtens* (1909)).

3. The company may enforce a provision in the articles, for example in *Hickman v Kent or Romney Marsh Sheepbreeders Association* (1915) the company was able to stop an action by a member and require that the dispute between it and its members be referred to arbitration as provided in the articles.

4.2.4 Enforcing 'outsider rights'

1. It is well established that no contract is created under s 33 between the company and an outsider, even a director. It is less clear whether 'outsider' rights can be enforced by a person bringing a claim as a member, on the basis that every member has the right to have the company's business conducted in accordance with the articles: see for example *Salmon v Quin & Axtens*.

2. This was suggested by Professor Lord Wedderburn in an important article in 1957 and has been the subject of academic debate since then.

3. It has also been suggested that if the provision in the articles relates to a constitutional matter, for example those listed above in section 4.2.3, then a member will be able to enforce the article as a contract, even if this indirectly enforces outsider rights.

4. But if the matter relates to an aspect of internal organisation or management of the company, for example the right to be paid a salary or the right to be the company's solicitor (*Eley v Positive Government Security Life Assurance Co Ltd* (1876)), then the provision will not be enforceable.

5. The provisions relating to unfair prejudice in Part 30 CA 2006 provide an alternative way for members and directors to enforce certain rights which might be unenforceable under s 33 (see further chapter 14) and in the case of small private companies shareholder agreements may be used to protect rights under the general law of contract.

4.3 Directors, the articles and extrinsic contracts

1. Under s 171 CA 2006, directors must act in accordance with the constitution but in their capacity as directors they have no contractual relationship with the company under s 33.

2. However, a company can make contracts with its directors and others, which expressly or impliedly incorporate terms contained in the articles, for example articles about directors' remuneration may be incorporated in a contract of service.

3. Where an article provides for the employment of a director but there is no contract, the court may imply an extrinsic contract (*Re New British Iron Co, ex parte Beckwith* (1898)).

4. These rights can be enforced against the company without relying on the articles, but alteration of the articles may vary the terms of the contract.

5. The articles can be altered at any time by special resolution, thus varying the terms of the contract, but terms cannot be altered retrospectively (*Swabey v Port Darwin Gold Mining Co* (1889)).

6. If provisions from the articles are incorporated into extrinsic contracts, alteration of the articles may result in breach of the extrinsic contract. A third party cannot prevent alteration of the articles, but in such cases the company may be liable to pay damages (*Southern Foundries (1926) Ltd v Shirlaw* (1940)).

4.4 Shareholder agreements

1. A shareholder agreement may be used in addition to the articles. Such an agreement may be made between all or some of the members and others including directors and is enforceable as an ordinary contract.

2. An example is *Russell v Northern Bank Development Corporation Ltd* (1992), where an agreement was made between all the shareholders and the company. It is held that an attempt by the company to restrict its statutory right to alter its articles was invalid but that the members were able to agree, by way of a shareholder agreement, to use their votes in a certain way (see also section 4.5.1 below).

3. Shareholder agreements will only bind the parties to it, so problems may arise on the transfer of shares as the new shareholder will not be bound by the agreement.

4. Because shareholder agreements require agreement by all members to be fully effective, they are generally only suitable for use by small private companies.

4.5 Alteration of articles

1. Other than in the case of an entrenched article, a company may alter its articles by:
   - special resolution (s 21 CA 2006);
   - agreement by all members (without a resolution) (*Cane v Jones* (1980)).

2. A company may not prevent its articles being altered, but it may entrench certain provisions by requiring something more than a special resolution to change them. Such entrenched provisions can only be included:

   ■ on formation of the company, or
   ■ after incorporation, by agreement of all the members of the company.

3. In the case of companies registered under previous legislation, certain provisions may have been included in the memorandum in order to make them more difficult to change. Such provisions will now be treated as if they were part of the articles (s 28 CA 2006) and may be treated as entrenched.

4. Notice of entrenchment must be given to the Registrar.

5. Provision for entrenchment does not prevent alteration of the articles by agreement of all the members or by order of the court.

6. Notice of alteration must be given to the Registrar within 15 days of alteration: s 26 CA 2006.

4.5.1 Restrictions on power to alter articles

Apart from the possibility of entrenchment, there are a number of restrictions on a company's power to alter its articles.

1. It has long been recognised that there are statutory limitations on amendment of articles (*Allen v Gold Reefs of West Africa Ltd* (1900)):

   ■ s 25 CA 2006: a member is not bound by a change which requires him/her to take more shares or in any way increase the member's liability, without the written agreement of the member.
   ■ ss 630–635 CA 2006: any alteration which varies class rights must follow the procedures laid down in these sections (see chapter 7, section 7.3 below).

2. A company may not include a provision in its articles that would restrict alteration of the articles (*Punt v Symons & Co* (1903)). It has further been held that a contract made by the company not to alter its articles is also unenforceable (*Russell v Northern Bank Development Corporation* (1992)). However, in the same case it was stated that it is possible for individual members to enter into a contract setting out how they might use their votes in certain situations.

3. Alterations to the articles are effective only if they are made *bona fide* for the benefit of the company as a whole. This principle, articulated in *Allen v Gold Reefs of West Africa Ltd* (1900), has been interpreted and further developed as the courts have applied it in different situations.

   ■ A member cannot challenge an alteration which was carried out *bona fide* for the benefit of the company as a whole, even if such alteration has affected the member's personal rights, as long as the altered article was intended to apply indiscriminately to all members: *Greenhalgh v Arderne Cinemas Ltd* (1951).

   ■ The court will generally accept the majority's *bona fide* view of what is for the benefit of the company as a whole, as long as the alteration is not one which no reasonable person could consider to be for the benefit of the company: *Shuttleworth v Cox Brothers & Co (Maidenhead) Ltd* (1927).

   ■ In some cases (for example *Greenhalgh*) the courts have sought to distinguish between the company as a separate entity and the company as an association of members and in deciding on the validity of certain amendments have applied a test based on whether the amendment was for the benefit of the 'individual hypothetical member'.

   ■ This concept has raised difficulties of application and other tests, such as the 'proper purpose' test, have been applied in other jurisdictions, notably Australia.

   ■ However, in *Citco Banking Corporation NV v Pusser's Ltd* (2007) the Privy Council confirmed that the benefit of the company as a separate commercial entity was the primary test in establishing the validity of an amendment to articles.

4. Cases in this area often involve minority shareholders challenging the decision of the majority and in many instances the protection available under ss 994–996 CA 2006 will provide a more effective remedy (see chapter 14).

5. Amendment of the articles may put the company in breach of a separate contract and liable to pay damages: *Southern Foundries (1926) Ltd v Shirlaw* (1940).

5

Company contracts

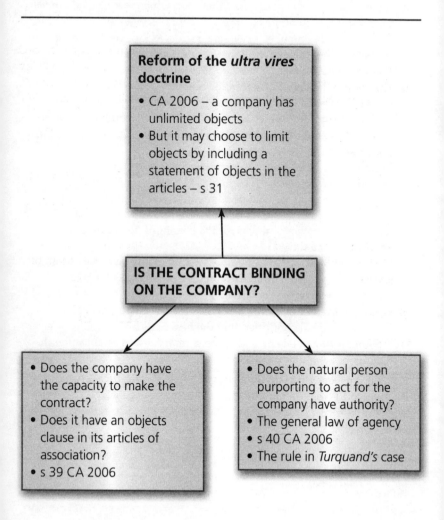

Reform of the *ultra vires* doctrine

- CA 2006 – a company has unlimited objects
- But it may choose to limit objects by including a statement of objects in the articles – s 31

IS THE CONTRACT BINDING ON THE COMPANY?

- Does the company have the capacity to make the contract?
- Does it have an objects clause in its articles of association?
- s 39 CA 2006

- Does the natural person purporting to act for the company have authority?
- The general law of agency
- s 40 CA 2006
- The rule in *Turquand's* case

5.1 Introduction

1. Under previous companies legislation, every company was required to include an objects clause in its memorandum of association, which in theory set out the purpose for which the company was formed and limited the activities of the company as described below.

2. The Companies Act 2006 (CA 2006) has changed the law in this respect. Section 31(1) provides 'Unless a company's articles specifically restrict the objects of the company, its objects are unrestricted'. A company is no longer obliged to include an objects clause in its constitution, in which case it will have full capacity to transact business.

3. However, a company may choose to restrict its objects by including a statement of objects in its articles of association.

4. Companies registered under previous Companies Acts will have statements of objects in their old-style memoranda, now treated as being a provision in their articles (s 28), unless they choose to remove these by special resolution.

5. Directors have a duty to act in accordance with the company's constitution (s 171 CA 2006), so where a company has a statement of objects, failure to act within the objects will be a breach of duty.

5.2 The *ultra vires* doctrine: historical perspective

5.2.1 The contractual capacity of companies

1. Since 1856 successive Companies Acts have required that an objects clause be included in the memorandum of association and this remained the case, with some modification as to the nature of the objects clause, until s 31 CA 2006 was brought into force.

2. The objects clause sets out the activities for which the company was formed and any activity outside this statement of objects is said to be *ultra vires* the company (outside the company's capacity). At common law any such transaction was void.

3. The reasons for the rule were:
   - that members are entitled to know the purpose for which their investment is to be used;

- it was supposed to protect creditors, who were deemed to know the contents of the memorandum.

4. The *ultra vires* rule was strengthened by the doctrine of constructive notice. Because the memorandum is a public document, anyone dealing with a company was deemed to know its contents, including its objects clause, so was deemed to know if a transaction was beyond the capacity of the company. This sometimes led to very harsh results (*Re Jon Beauforte (London) Ltd* (1953)).

5. There is a tension between the need to ensure that the company's property is used for the benefit of the members, and the need not to place undue constraints on the directors' freedom to take the company forward. The objects clause and the *ultra vires* doctrine achieved the former at common law, but not the latter. Companies found the doctrine restrictive and ingenious draftsmen found ways around it.

6. The previous strictness of the *ultra vires* doctrine was ameliorated, first by s 9 of the European Communities Act 1972, consolidated as s 35 CA 1985, and then by the Companies Act 1989, which substituted a new s 35 in the 1985 Act. The principle is still relevant, in companies with restricted objects, as an internal mechanism which limits the directors' authority to enter into an *ultra vires* transaction.

5.2.2 Development of the law

1. In *Ashbury Railway Carriage & Iron Co Ltd v Riche* (1875) the House of Lords held that a company did not have the capacity to enter into a contract outside the objects clause and therefore such a contract could not be enforced by either party. One consequence of this was that a company could escape liability when it had acted outside its objects clause.

2. It became commonplace for companies to include long objects clauses with a number of separate clauses followed by a clause to the effect that each and every paragraph contained a separate object of the company – known as a *Cotman v Brougham* clause (*Cotman v Brougham* (1918)).

3. Another device used by companies was the 'subjective' objects clause, considered by the court in *Bell Houses v City Wall Properties Ltd* (1966). Two main objects were followed by a clause stating that the company had capacity 'to carry on any other trade or business whatsoever which can, in the opinion of the board of directors, be advantageously

carried on by the company in connection with or ancillary to any of the above businesses or the general business of the company'. The law was further complicated by the distinction found by the judges between objects and powers (*Re Introductions* (1968); *Re Horsley & Weight Ltd* (1982)).

4. In *Rolled Steel Products (Holdings) Ltd v British Steel Corporation* (1986) the Court of Appeal reviewed and clarified the law, holding that where the directors exercise a power stated in the objects clause that is reasonably incidental to the company's substantive objects, this will be within the capacity of the company unless it amounts to a breach of fiduciary duty and the third party has knowledge of this.

5.3 Reform

5.3.1 Reform prior to 2006 Act

1. The *ultra vires* rule has been the subject of controversy over a long period. Its application allowed companies to avoid transactions, often producing harsh results for third parties. Security of transaction for those dealing with companies has been an important objective in the reform of the law in this area.

2. In 1945 the Cohen Committee (Cmd 6659) recommended that a company should have the same capacity to enter into transactions as an individual as regards third parties. Different recommendations for reform were made by the Jenkins Committee (CMND 1749) in 1962 and the Prentice Report (1986) but none of these was implemented at the time.

3. In 1973, when the United Kingdom's entry into the EEC made it necessary to comply with Art 9 of the First Company Law Directive. Section 9(1) of the European Communities Act 1972 (consolidated as s 35 Companies Act 1985) provided: 'In favour of a person dealing with a company in good faith, any transaction decided on by the directors shall be deemed to be one which it is within the capacity of the company to enter into, and the power of the directors to bind the company shall be deemed to be free of any limitation under the memorandum or articles of association'.

4. This provision gave rise to considerable uncertainty. The main issues were the meaning of 'good faith' and whether the term 'directors'

should be interpreted as the board of directors or whether it covered a single director. The drive for reform continued.

5. The Companies Act 1989 amended s 35 of the Companies Act 1985, addressing some of the difficulties and providing that the validity of an act done by a company shall not be called into question on the ground of lack of capacity by reason of anything in the company's memorandum (s 35(1)).

6. This section effectively abolished the *ultra vires* rule as far as transactions between the company and third parties were concerned, but the objects clause and the *ultra vires* doctrine still potentially had application with respect to the internal management of the company.

7. The section provided that a member could bring proceedings to stop the company from carrying out an act which, but for s 35, would be beyond the company's capacity, unless the company was under a legal obligation as a result of the act (s 35(2)). It provided further that directors have a duty to act within their powers as set out in the memorandum (s 35(3)).

8. The 1989 Act also inserted s 3A which allowed a company to simply state its object as being 'to carry on business as a general commercial company'. However, this short-form objects clause was not widely adopted in practice.

5.3.2 Companies Act 2006

1. All companies registered under the 2006 Act will have unlimited objects, unless a clause specifically restricting a company's objects is included in the articles: s 31(1). Companies registered under earlier Acts may still have a statement of objects in their old-style memoranda.

2. Section 31(2) and (3) provides that any change to a company's articles so as to add, remove or alter a statement of objects must be notified to the Registrar.

3. Section 39 re-enacts s 35(1) CA 1985, except that the word 'constitution' replaces 'memorandum'. The section provides that the validity of an act done by a company should not be called into question by reason of anything in the company's constitution.

4. There is no equivalent in the 2006 Act of s 35(2) and (3) CA 1985. These sections were considered unnecessary because of the fact that companies will have unlimited objects, unless expressly restricted,

together with the fact that s 171 places a duty on directors to abide by the constitution.

5.4 Agency principles and company law

5.4.1 Introduction: the general law of agency

1. Separate legal personality ensures that a company can contract with others, but being an artificial person, a company can only act through agents.

2. CA 2006 refers to 'an act done by the company'. The law of agency and ss 40–41 CA 2006 must be considered in deciding when an act is done by a company.

3. It is a general rule that, with some statutory exceptions, a person can only enforce a contract if he or she is a party to it. This is the doctrine of privity of contract.

4. The law of agency is a major common law exception to this rule and enables a person with the appropriate authority (the agent) to create a contract that binds his or her principal. Most commercial transactions are carried out through the law of agency.

5. In the law of agency, an agent will only be able to make a contract which binds the principal if the agent is acting within the authority given to him by the principal. A company's articles will usually give directors the authority to manage the company and directors will in turn delegate authority to others within the company to make contracts that bind the company.

5.4.2 Types of authority

Authority may be either actual or ostensible (sometimes called apparent authority).

1. **Actual authority** is described by Lord Diplock in *Freeman & Lockyer v Buckhurst Properties (Mangal) Ltd* (1964) as 'a legal relationship between the principal and the agent created by a consensual agreement to which they alone are the parties'. It is the authority that is given to the agent by the principal by way of a contact which sets out the scope of that authority. This may be done expressly in writing or orally, in which case it is known as express actual authority. It is also

possible for the principal to confer on the agent implied actual authority. This may arise:

- when an agent has express authority to perform a certain task, authority may be implied by virtue of the fact that it is necessary to enable the agent to complete the task;
- when implied authority is inferred by the conduct of the principal, for example a person appointed to a certain position may have implied actual authority to carry out the tasks usually associated with that position (*Hely Hutchinson v Brayhead Ltd* (1967)).

Both express and implied actual authority are conferred on the agent by the principal and the perceptions of the third party contactor are irrelevant.

2. **Ostensible (or apparent) authority** is the authority which the agent appears to the third party contractor to have by virtue of a representation made by the principal: *Freeman & Lockyer v Buckhurst Properties (Mangal) Ltd* (1964). In this case Lord Diplock set out four requirements for ostensible authority:

   (a) There must be a representation made to the third party by words or conduct that the agent has authority. In other words, the company must act in such a way that it appears to the third party that the agent has authority.

   (b) The representation must be made by the principal or by persons who had actual authority.

   (c) The third party must rely on the representation in entering into the contract.

   (d) The company must have capacity to enter into the contract. The provisions now contained in s 39 and s 40 CA 2006 mean that this requirement is no longer relevant.

3. In *Armagas Ltd v Mundogas SA* (1986), Lord Keith of Kinkel said 'Ostensible authority comes about where the principal, by words or conduct, has represented that the agent has the requisite actual authority, and the party dealing with the agent has entered into a contract with him in reliance on that representation'. It is important to note that ostensible authority depends on the perceptions of the third party contractor, not on the intentions of the principal. Further, an agent cannot represent himself as having authority: representation must come from the principal.

4. Ostensible authority may be conferred by a particular job title, for example company secretary (*Panorama Developments v Fidelis Furnishing*

Fabrics (1971)), and in certain circumstances to directors with particular responsibilities, such as a Finance Director.

5. The company may withdraw authority from a person who has acted with ostensible authority but third parties may continue to rely on the representation until they are notified of the change: *AMB Generali Holding AG v Manches* (2005).

6. An important difference between actual and ostensible authority is that a company cannot rely on ostensible authority of an agent to enforce a contract made outside its authority: *Re Quintox Ltd No 2* (1990).

5.5 Section 40 Companies Act 2006

5.5.1 The board of directors

1. Articles of association usually provide that the company's business shall be managed by the board of directors (Art 3 in the model articles for both public companies and private companies limited by shares) so all powers of management are delegated to the board. In this way the company appoints its agents and gives them authority.

2. The directors of a company have actual authority to bind the company if they are acting for the company or, in the case of a company with restricted objects, for the purpose of attaining the company's objects (*Rolled Steel Products (Holdings) Ltd v British Steel Corporation* (1986)).

3. The directors, acting as a board, are agents of the company and a third party can usually rely on the actions of the directors in accordance with the ordinary principles of the law of agency.

4. However, difficulties may arise if the authority of the board is limited in some way by the company's constitution; for example the general meeting may have the right to veto the sale of certain assets. In such situations, s 40 CA 2006 applies and will provide security of contract to the third party.

5. The board of directors may delegate authority to others. Such delegation, to a single director, employees or others, is common practice.

5.5.2 The scope of s 40

1. Section 40 CA 2006 deals with the authority of directors to bind the company and, like s 39, it is intended to increase the security of persons dealing with a company.

2. Section 40 CA 2006 provides:

   '(1) In favour of a person dealing with a company in good faith, the power of the directors to bind the company, or to authorise others to do so, is deemed to be free of any limitation under the company's constitution.'

3. The meaning of 'person' in this section was considered in *Smith v Henniker-Major & Co* (2002), a case brought under the predecessor to s 40 (s 35A CA 1985). The claimant was a director of the company and the court considered whether a director of the company could rely on the section. It was held that in some circumstances a director would be covered by the section, but that a director who had taken part without authority in causing the company to enter into the transaction (as in this case) could not rely on s 40 to enforce it.

4. The decision to enter into the transaction in this case was made by an inquorate board and the question also arose whether the section covered procedural irregularities as well as limitations under the constitution. The Court of Appeal was divided on the issue, which remains unresolved.

5. 'Dealing' covers any transaction or act to which the company is a party (s 40(2)(a)), overruling the decision in *International Sales and Agencies v Marcus* (1982).

6. Under s 40(2)(b) a person dealing with a company:

   (i)   is not bound to enquire as to any limitation on the powers of the directors to bind the company or authorise others to do so;

   (ii) is presumed to have acted in good faith unless the contrary is proved (the burden of proving bad faith is placed on the company);

   (iii) is not to be regarded as acting in bad faith by reason only of his knowing that an act is beyond the powers of the directors under the company's constitution.

Note that s 40(2)(b)(i) above does not protect a contractor when the circumstances suggest that enquiries about other matters should have been made, for example whether the person who purported to act for the company had authority to do so: *Wrexham Associated Football Club Ltd v Crucialmove Ltd* (2007).

7. Section 40(3) provides that limitations on the directors' power under the company's constitution include limitations deriving from:

   (i)   a resolution of the company or any class of shareholder; and

(ii) any agreement between the members of the company or any class of shareholder.

8. A member can bring proceedings to restrain an act which is beyond the powers of the directors, unless the act has given rise to legal obligations (s 40(4)).

9. The section does not affect any liability incurred by the directors, or other person, as a result of exceeding their powers (s 40(5)).

10. These provisions apply only to 'a person dealing with the company' – the company itself cannot enforce a contract entered without actual authority unless it ratifies the transaction.

5.5.3 Section 41: Transactions involving directors

1. Section 41 CA 2006 restricts the protection given to persons dealing with a company in certain circumstances.

2. The transaction is voidable by the company and the person concerned is liable to account to the company for any profit and to indemnify the company for any loss arising from the contract when the parties to the transaction include:
   - a director of the company or its holding company;
   - a person connected with such a director;
   - a person connected with a company with whom such a director is associated.

3. The transaction will not be voidable in the following circumstances:
   - if restitution is no longer possible;
   - if the company is indemnified for any loss;
   - if avoidance of the transaction would affect rights that have been acquired *bona fide*, for value and without notice that the directors had exceeded their powers;
   - if the transaction is ratified by the company in general meeting.

5.5.4 Other agents

1. Under s 40 CA 2006, neither the authority of the board to bind the company nor its ability to authorise others to do so can be called into question in favour of a person dealing with the company in good faith.

2. Thus the board may delegate authority to others, for example to a single director or an employee of the company. But in order to decide whether the board has in fact given authority to another person

application of the general law of agency will be necessary, as discussed above in section 5.4.

5.6 The indoor management rule

5.6.1 The rule in *Turquand's* case

1. The application of agency rules has always caused some difficulties in company law, particularly in the context of limitations on the authority of directors imposed by the company's constitution.

2. This is because persons dealing with a company will not usually be aware of such limitations and the doctrine of constructive notice exacerbated the problem, since anyone dealing with a company was deemed to know the contents of the memorandum and articles of association, whether or not he or she had actually seen these documents.

3. The rule in *Turquand's* case (the indoor management rule) developed alongside the doctrine of constructive notice and mitigates its effect.

4. Under this rule, where:
   - the directors have power to bind the company, but certain preliminaries must be gone through, and
   - there are no suspicious circumstances,

   A person dealing with a company is entitled to assume that all matters of internal procedure have been complied with (*Royal British Bank v Turquand* (1876); *Mahoney v East Holyford Mining Company* (1875); *Rolled Steel Products (Holdings) Ltd v British Steel Corporation* (1982)).

5. However, if a contract is made without authority, a director of the company who knew or ought to have known of the lack of authority cannot rely on the indoor management rule: *Morris v Kanssen* (1946).

5.6.2 Is the rule in *Turquand's* case still relevant?

1. Section 40 CA 2006 is wider than the rule in *Turquand's* case since knowledge of a defect prevents the third party contractor from relying on *Turquand* (*Morris v Kanssen* (1946)), while knowledge of limitations on directors' powers does not stop a third party from relying on s 40. The introduction of s 40 (and its predecessors) has largely subsumed the rule in *Turquand's* case.

2. However, the rule may still have application where the limitation on the board's power to act is not strictly constitutional, such as when a decision to enter into a transaction is made by an inquorate board: *Smith v Henniker-Major & Co* (2002). But note that in this case the person seeking to enforce the contract was a director of the company and the rule in *Turquand's* case does not apply where if the person seeking to rely on it knew or should have known of the irregularity.

6

Meetings and resolutions

Decisions of members expressed in resolutions
- Ordinary resolution – simple majority required
- Special resolution – 75% of vote

The role of meetings and resolutions in company decision-making
- Different requirements for public and private companies
- Part 13 CA 2006

Written resolutions – s288 'a resolution of a private company that has been proposed and passed in accordance with Part 13, chapter 2'
- Procedure set out in ss 291–292
- Must be sent to all eligible members
- The resolution is passed when the necessary majority of eligible members have signified agreement

MEETINGS AND RESOLUTIONS

Meetings
- Private companies not required to hold annual general meetings unless their articles state otherwise
- Public companies must hold annual general meeting within six months of end of their financial year
- Any company may call a general meeting
- A meeting is required to remove a director or auditor before end of term of office

Conduct of meetings

Notice:
- 21 days for AGM
- 14 days for other general meeting unless articles provide otherwise
- May be given in hard copy, by email or by website

Quorum:
- At common law – one person cannot constitute a meeting (*Sharp v Dawes* (1876))
- s 318 – one qualifying person in company with one member, two in any other case

Voting:
- Show of hands – each member has one vote
- Poll – each member has a vote for every share
- Members may appoint proxies to attend and vote in their place

6.1 Introduction

6.1.1 The role of meetings and resolutions

1. A company, as an artificial person, is able to act only through its agents. By appointing the board of directors the shareholders in general meeting appoint agents to act for the company. The articles of association generally provide that the business of the company shall be conducted by the board of directors.

2. Usually, the role of shareholders in general meeting is a residual one, but note:
   - the shareholders can give directions to the board by special resolution;
   - certain statutory provisions, and sometimes the articles themselves, require the authority of shareholders before action can be taken by the board;
   - shareholders in general meeting may appoint the directors, in accordance with the company's articles, and under s 168 Companies Act 2006 they have power to remove directors by ordinary resolution.

3. Shareholder meetings and written resolutions are the mechanisms by which shareholders exercise those decision-making rights that are reserved to the company by the Companies Act 2006 (CA 2006).

4. A formal mechanism for exchanging information and making certain important decisions is needed and, in the case of public companies, the meeting is the focus of corporate decision-making by the shareholders and accountability on the part of the directors.

6.1.2 Public and private companies

1. The annual general meeting (AGM) has long been recognised as an unsatisfactory forum for the exchange of views and decision-making in modern companies, although the reasons for this differ between public companies on the one hand and private companies on the other.

2. Public companies often have very large numbers of shareholders, some of whom are small private investors, while others are institutional shareholders.
   - Annual general meetings tend to be poorly attended and private investors tend to have little influence on decisions taken.

- Institutional shareholders with large holdings of shares often exercise their influence outside the annual general meetings.

3. Shareholders in private companies tend to be fewer in number and less widely dispersed. In the case of small private companies (quasi-partnerships) the shareholders may all themselves be directors and work closely together in running the company, so the need for a formal AGM has been questioned.

4. Part 13 of the CA 2006 replaces Part 11, Chapter 4 of the CA 1985 and contains the provisions relating to meetings and resolutions. There are a number of amendments, many of which were designed to enhance the involvement of shareholders in public companies and to reduce the administrative burden on private companies.

5. Under CA 1985 a private company was able to dispense with annual general meetings, but was required to pass a resolution if it wished to do so. CA 2006 reverses the situation and there is now no requirement for a private company to hold annual general meetings, unless it includes a provision in its articles requiring such meetings.

6. Decisions in private companies, which under CA 1985 were assumed to be taken by resolution in general meeting, will under the CA 2006 be taken by written resolution without the need for a meeting.

7. A private company is still required to hold a general meeting in order to remove a director or to dismiss an auditor before the end of his term of office. Also, a general meeting can be called by the directors at any time or by members representing 10% of the voting shares, or 5% if it is more than 12 months since the last shareholder meeting.

6.2 Resolutions

Decisions of the company made by members are expressed in resolutions, either passed at a general meeting in the case of a public company, or by the written resolution procedure in the case of a private company with no constitutional requirement to hold AGMs.

6.2.1 Ordinary resolutions

1. An ordinary resolution is defined by s 282(1) CA 2006 as one that is passed with a simple majority.
   (a) In the case of a written resolution this requires a simple majority of

the total voting rights of eligible members (s 282(2)). The written resolution procedure is available only to private companies.

(b) A resolution passed at a meeting on a show of hands requires a simple majority of members who, being entitled to do so, vote in person on the resolution, and persons who vote as duly appointed proxies (s 282(3)).

(c) On a poll a resolution is passed by a simple majority of the total voting rights of members who vote in person or by proxy (s 282(4)).

2. Unless otherwise stipulated in the Companies Act or in the company's constitution, company decisions can be taken by ordinary resolution.

3. Note in particular that an ordinary resolution is required to remove directors (s 168).

6.2.2 Special resolutions

1. A special resolution is defined by s 283(1) as one that is passed by not less than 75%.

(a) s 283(2) provides that in the case of a written resolution this means not less than 75% of the total voting rights of eligible members.

(b) Under s 283(3) a resolution is not a special resolution unless it is stated that it is proposed as a special resolution and it is one that can only be passed as a special resolution.

(c) s 283(4) provides that a special resolution passed at a meeting on a show of hands requires 75% of members who, being entitled to do so, vote in person on the resolution and those who vote as duly appointed proxies.

(d) s 283(5) provides that on a poll taken at a meeting a special resolution is passed by a majority of not less than 75% of the total voting rights of members who, being entitled to do so, vote on the resolution.

2. Under CA 2006 a special resolution is required for a large number of purposes, including:

■ to alter the articles of association (s 21));
■ to change a company's name, unless the company's articles provide for another method (s 77);
■ to approve a reduction of capital (s 641(1)).

3. The Insolvency Act 1986 requires a special resolution, for example:

■ to resolve that the company should be wound up voluntarily (s 84(1)(b));

- in a members' voluntary liquidation, to approve the transfer of shares to another company (s 110(3));
- to resolve to petition for a compulsory winding up (s 122(1)(a)).

6.2.3 Unanimous assent of all members

1. It is well established that the unanimous agreement of all members is effective, even if a meeting is not held: *Cane v Jones* (1981); *Re Duomatic* (1969). Such agreement must be notified to the register under s 30 CA 2006.

2. It should be noted, however, that unanimous assent will not be effective where a statutory provision requires more than just a resolution, for example where a particular procedure is required as for the removal of a director or auditor.

6.3 Written resolutions

1. A written resolution is defined in s 288 CA 2006 as 'a resolution of a private company that has been proposed and passed in accordance with Chapter 2, Part 13'. A written resolution may be proposed by the directors or by members.

2. Under CA 1985 a written resolution required the unanimous support of all members. This is no longer the case – see sections 6.2.1 and 6.2.2 above.

3. The procedure for written resolutions proposed by the directors is set out in some detail in s 291 CA 2006:
   (a) The resolution must be sent to every eligible member by one or a combination of the following:
   - in hard copy;
   - by email;
   - by the website.
   (b) A company using email or the website must have the consent of shareholders to use these forms of communication (s 1144(2) and Schedule 5).
   (c) The resolution must be accompanied by a statement setting out how a shareholder must signify agreement and by notification of the date by which the resolution must be passed if it is not to lapse. Section 297 provides that the period in which agreement must be signified is as specified in the articles, or if no period is specified, 28 days beginning with the circulation date.

(d) A resolution is passed as soon as the necessary majority of eligible members have signified agreement. It will lapse if it is not passed before the end of the period specified in the articles or, if none is specified, 28 days.

4. Sections 292–295 deal with the procedure for written resolutions proposed by members.

   (a) Shareholders who hold 5% of the voting rights can require the directors to circulate a proposed resolution. Directors are not required to circulate a resolution if it would be ineffective even if passed, if it is defamatory or if it is frivolous or vexatious.

   (b) Members may require a statement of not more than 1,000 words to be sent with the proposed resolution.

   (c) The members requiring circulation are liable to pay the expenses.

6.4 Meetings

6.4.1 Meetings under CA 2006

1. Public companies are required under s 336(1) to hold an annual general meeting within six months of the end of their financial year. The main purpose of an AGM is to consider the accounts and reports of the auditors and directors; to declare any dividend and to elect directors and auditors. Section 337 provides that the notice calling an AGM must state that it is an annual general meeting.

2. Private companies are not required by the Act to hold an AGM, but must do so if their articles so provide.

3. A general meeting can be called by all companies and is required in order to remove a director or dismiss an auditor before the end of his term of office.

4. Directors have the power to call a general meeting under s 302. The concept of the extraordinary general meeting has been abolished by the CA 2006.

5. Under s 303 directors must call a general meeting if requested:

   (a) in the case of a public company, by members holding 10% of the voting rights;

   (b) in the case of a private company, by members holding 10% of the voting rights, or 5% if a general meeting has not been held for more than 12 months.

6. Class meetings must be held in certain circumstances. This is a meeting open to members of a particular class of shareholders or creditors (see chapters 7 and 16).

6.4.2 Conduct of meetings

1. Notice
   (a) Members must be given 21 days notice for an AGM of a public company unless all members entitled to attend and vote agree to a shorter period: ss 307(2) and 337(2).
   (b) 14 days notice is required for any other general meeting, unless the articles specify a longer period: s 307(1)–(3).
   (c) Special notice of 28 days is required for a resolution at an AGM to remove an auditor from office, or providing that a retiring auditor will not be re-appointed (ss 511, 514, 515), or to remove a director under s 168.
   (d) No business may be brought to a meeting unless notice has been given.
   (e) Notice may be given in hard copy, electronic form or by a website, or by a combination. Electronic form and the website may be used if a member has agreed that notice may be given in that way. If the website is used, members who have agreed to receive notice in that way must be notified that notice has been posted.

2. Quorum
   (a) At common law, one person cannot constitute a meeting: *Sharp v Dawes* (1876); *Re London Flats Ltd* (1969). However, this has been varied by the Companies Act, for example:
      ■ class meetings where there is only one member of the class;
      ■ under s 306 CA 2006 the court may order a meeting to be held and fix the quorum at one (*Re El Sombrero Ltd* (1958); *Re Sticky Fingers Restaurant Ltd* (1992)).
   (b) Section 318 CA 2006 provides that the quorum for a valid meeting is one 'qualifying person' in a company with only one member and two in any other case, unless the articles provide otherwise. A qualifying person is a member, the representative of a corporate member or a proxy.
   (c) No business can be done unless a quorum is present.

3. Voting
   (a) Generally voting at general meetings is by show of hands with each member having one vote.

(b) A poll may be demanded in accordance with the statute and the articles, in which case a written record is kept and each member has a vote for every share held: s 284.

(c) Section 321 lays down minimum requirements as to who may demand a poll at general meetings.

(d) Section 322 provides that on a poll at a general meeting a member who is entitled to more than one vote need not cast all his votes in the same way.

(e) If a poll is held at a general meeting of a quoted company the results must be published on the company's website in accordance with s 341.

(f) Members of a quoted company may also require directors to provide an independent report on any poll taken at an AGM.

(g) These measures are designed to enhance transparency.

4. **Proxies**

   (a) A member can appoint a proxy to attend, speak and vote at a meeting. A proxy may vote on both a show of hands and a poll.

   (b) Section 323 allows a corporate member to appoint a human representative with the same powers as an individual member.

5. Under s 355(2) records of meetings and resolutions must be kept for 10 years from the date of the resolution, meeting or decision. Under previous legislation there was no statutory requirement.

6. A meeting can be held by telephone (*Re Associated Colour Laboratories Ltd* (1970)).

7. A meeting can be held in different rooms with audio-visual links between them (*Byng v London Life Association Ltd* (1990)).

7

Shares

The nature of shares:

A **share** is a form of property – it does not give the shareholder an interest in the assets of the company

Rights depend on terms of issue of a particular class of shares. Shareholders generally have:
- a right to vote
- a right to dividends when declared
- a right to return of contributed capital and surplus assets on winding up.

Class rights

- Different classes of share carry different rights
- Class rights only arise when a company has more than one class of share
- Variation of class rights – procedure under ss 630–633 CA 2006

SHARES

Offering shares to the public

- Shares in a **public company** may be offered to the public
- Transfer of shares in a **private company** may be restricted by the company's constitution
- The offer of shares to the public is regulated to ensure a fair market and protect investors

7.1 Shares

7.1.1 The nature of shares

1. A company can raise capital either by issuing equity securities (shares) or by borrowing.

2. Shareholders undertake to contribute an agreed amount of capital to the company and, if the company is limited by shares, this is then the limit of the shareholders' liability.

3. A share is a way of measuring each member's interest in the company. So if a company has an authorised and issued share capital of £10,000 divided into £1 ordinary shares and shareholder A owns 1,000 shares, he will have a 10% interest in the company.

4. In *Borlands Trustee v Steel Bros & Co Ltd* (1901) Farwell J said: 'The share is the interest of the shareholder in the company measured by a sum of money, for the purpose of liability in the first place, and interest in the second, but also of a series of mutual covenants entered into by all the shareholders *inter se* in accordance with [s 33 CA 2006]'.

7.1.2 Effects of shareholding

- Shareholders have a right to a distribution of profits by way of a dividend declared on the shares.
- Except in the case of non-voting shares, each shareholder has the right to vote.
- If the company is wound up when not insolvent, capital is returned to members in proportion to their shareholding.
- Shares are transferable and may, in the case of a plc, be offered to the public. In a private company there may be restrictions on the transfer of shares if so provided in the articles.
- Shareholders have rights and obligations as defined in the company's constitution by virtue of s 33 of the Companies Act 2006 (CA 2006) (see chapter 4, section 4.2 above).

7.1.3 Share capital

1. Under s 9(4) CA 2006 an application for registration of a company that is to have a share capital must contain a statement of share capital and initial holdings.

2. Section 542 provides that all shares must, as under the 1985 Act, have a fixed nominal value.

3. Section 10 provides that the statement of share capital must give details of:
   - the total number of shares to be taken by the subscribers on formation;
   - the aggregate nominal value of those shares;
   - details with respect to each class of share;
   - the amount to be paid and the amount (if any) unpaid on each share. Details of the subscribers will also have to be given as well as the number, nominal value and class of share taken by each subscriber and the amount paid up.

4. A company may issue different classes of shares, each class having different rights (see section 7.3 below).

5. The concept of authorised share capital is abolished by the CA 2006.

6. *Paid up share capital* is the amount actually contributed to the share capital of the company, excluding any premium and excluding calls made but not yet paid. If partly paid shares are issued, the shareholder will pay part of the price when the shares are issued and will be liable to pay the remainder at some time in the future.

7. *Called up share capital* is the total amount already paid plus any share capital that must be paid on a future date as specified in the articles or terms of allotment.

7.1.4 Alteration of share capital

Under s 617 CA 2006 share capital may be altered in a number of ways, including:
   - new shares may be allotted to increase the share capital;
   - reduction of capital (see chapter 8);
   - subdivision;
   - consolidation;
   - redenomination, by which the shares are denominated in a different currency. Associated with this, capital may be reduced by up to 10% in order to arrive at a sensible, rounded amount.

The Act sets out detailed provisions associated with all of these procedures.

7.1.5 Types of share

1. *Ordinary shares* will usually carry one vote per share on a poll. The dividend is that recommended by the directors, and the amount payable on a distribution of assets on a winding up is proportional to the nominal value of the shares.

2. *Preference* shares usually entitle the holders to a dividend of a fixed amount per share to be paid in priority to other shareholders. Note, however, that there is no entitlement until the dividend is declared. Preference shares may be:

   ■ cumulative: if the dividend is not paid in one year, then the shareholder will be entitled to receive the arrears from profits in subsequent years. Unless the articles or terms of issue provide otherwise, preference shares are cumulative.

   ■ non-cumulative: the dividend will lapse if the company is unable to pay it in any one year.

   Preference shares may also entitle the holder to prior return of capital on a winding up where the company is solvent.

3. *Deferred shares* (sometimes called *founders' shares*) are now rare. Promoters used to take shares which would not qualify for a dividend until the ordinary shareholders had received one.

4. *Redeemable shares* are issued with a provision that they may be bought back by the company at a later date, at the option of either the company or the shareholder.

5. *Non-voting shares* carry similar rights to ordinary shares, but no right to vote.

7.2 Allotment of shares

7.2.1 Allotment and issue

1. Shares are allotted when a person acquires the unconditional right to be entered in the register of members in respect of that share (s 558 CA 2006).

2. Shares are issued when the holder's name is entered in the register of members (*Re Heaton's Steel and Iron Co, Blythe's Case* (1876); *National Westminster Bank plc v Inland Revenue Commissioners* (1995)).

3. Members have some control over how directors allot new shares. In principle, directors may not allot shares (except in specified circumstances) unless they have authority to do so either by the articles or by ordinary resolution. The CA 2006 provides:

   (a) s 550 – in the case of a private company with only one class of shares the directors will have unrestricted power to allot new shares unless there are restrictions in the articles.

   (b) s 551(1) – in the case of any other company the directors cannot allot new shares unless they are authorised to do so either by the articles or by ordinary resolution. A public company cannot give such authority for a period of more than five years at any one time.

   (c) s 551(8) – authority to allot shares can be given, varied, revoked or renewed by ordinary resolution, even if such authority is provided by the articles.

   (d) resolutions authorising directors to allot shares and resolutions revoking authority must be notified to the Registrar.

7.2.2 Payment for shares

1. Shares may be issued in exchange for cash or for other forms of property, for example in a takeover the offeror company may offer its shares in return for shares in the offeree company.

7.2.3 Pre-emption rights

1. Further capital can be raised by way of a rights issue.

2. A member's influence within a company depends upon the proportion of shares held. The provisions governing pre-emption rights are complex and are contained in ss 561–573 CA 2006. They aim to ensure that the interests of existing shareholders are not diluted, while allowing for certain exceptions to the general rule and also allowing companies to disapply the provision.

   (a) s 561 provides that before any equity securities are allotted in exchange for a cash contribution, they should first be offered to existing shareholders on the same or more favourable terms.

   (b) s 562 provides that the offer must be communicated to shareholders and sets out how this should be done.

   (c) s 563 – failure to comply with the above sections is a criminal offence and the company and any officer in default must compensate shareholders to whom the offer should have been made.

(d) ss 564–566 provide for certain exceptions:
- allotment of bonus shares;
- where shares are issued for a non-cash consideration;
- where shares are held under an employees' share scheme.

(e) s 569 provides that in the case of private company with only one class of share the right of pre-emption may be excluded.

(f) Under s 570 if directors of any public or private company are generally authorised under s 551 to allot shares, they may be given power in the articles or by special resolution to allot new shares as if s 561 does not apply.

(g) s 571 allows for the disapplication of s 561 by special resolution in relation to a specific allotment of equity securities.

7.3 Class rights

7.3.1 General details

1. Companies may issue shares such as ordinary shares or preference shares, with different rights attached to them.

2. Different classes of share will have different rights attached to them, which may be set out in the articles of association, terms of issue or unanimous shareholder agreement.

3. Section 21 of the CA 2006 provides that, subject to the provisions of the Act and to conditions contained in the articles, a company may, by special resolution, alter its articles of association. A company cannot deprive itself of its statutory power to alter the articles (*Allen v Gold Reefs of West Africa Ltd* (1900)), but if any alteration involves the variation of class rights then ss 630–635 (designed to give protection to minorities in relation to their class rights) will apply and such rights can only be varied if the proper procedures are followed.

4. Class rights will only arise if the company has more than one class of share.

5. There is no statutory definition of a class right but the nature of class rights was considered in *Cumbrian Newspapers Group Ltd v Cumberland and Westmorland Herald Newspaper and Printing Co Ltd* (1986). It was held that rights and benefits may be:
- rights annexed to particular shares such as the right to a dividend or voting rights;

- rights conferred on individuals not in their capacity as members, i.e. outsider rights. These are not class rights;
- rights conferred on individuals in their capacity as members, but not attached to shares.

The first and third categories only may be described as class rights.

7.3.2 Variation of class rights

1. The general rule is that rights of one class of shareholders should not be altered by another class by just amending the articles.

2. CA 2006 restated the previous law with some amendments intended to simplify the procedure and to take into account the fact that the articles are the main constitutional document under the 2006 Act. It also extended protection of class rights to companies without a share capital.

7.3.3 Meaning of 'variation of rights'

1. The legislation does not make it clear what is meant by 'variation of class rights'.

2. The courts have taken a restrictive view and have sought to distinguish between the rights themselves and the 'enjoyment of the rights'.

3. It may thus be possible to make rights less effective without any technical 'variation' of rights (*White v Bristol Aeroplane Co* (1953); *Greenhalgh v Arderne Cinemas* (1946)).

7.3.4 Procedure for variation

1. Section 630 sets out the procedure for companies with a share capital.

2. If the articles provide for a variation of rights procedure, this must be complied with (s 630(2)(a)). Provision in the articles may be more or less demanding than the statutory procedure.

3. Neither the model articles for public companies nor those for private companies limited by shares make provision for the variation of class rights.

4. In the absence of any procedure in the articles, class rights may only be varied with the consent of the members of that class.

5. Consent can be given:

- by the holders of at least three quarters of the nominal value of the issued shares in that class signifying their agreement in writing (s 630(4)(a)), or
- by special resolution passed at a separate general meeting of that class (s 630(4)(b)).

6. Section 631 sets out the procedure required for companies without a share capital. In this case, in the absence of any provision in the articles, consent may be given:
   - in writing by three quarters of the membership of that class (s 631(4)(a)), or
   - by special resolution passed at a separate general meeting of that class (s 631(4)(b)).

7. Section 633 gives dissenting members of a class who hold not less than 15% of shares of that class the right to apply to the court to have the variation cancelled. However, they must act within 21 days of the variation, which may cause difficulties in large companies.

8. The court may disallow the variation if it can be shown that the variation would unfairly prejudice the class. Otherwise the court must confirm the variation.

7.4 Offering shares to the public

7.4.1 Introduction

1. Only a public company may offer its shares to the public. Most companies are set up as private companies, so if a company wishes to offer its shares more widely it will have to 'go public'. There are a number of reasons why a company may wish to do this, including to enable the company to raise capital from new investors and to provide a market for existing shareholders to sell their shares. Because there is a ready market for the sale of the shares, public companies are attractive to investors.

2. There are also disadvantages. A public company is subject to more rigorous disclosure requirements and much greater public scrutiny by the press. It may also be an easier target for a takeover bid.

3. Previously, under s 81 CA 1985, a private company committed an offence if it offered shares to the public, but this is no longer the case under the Companies Act 2006.

7.4.2 Listing and markets

1. The public offer of shares is subject to regulation under the Financial Services and Markets Act (FSMA) 2000. The purpose of regulation is to ensure that there is investor confidence in the markets on which shares can be traded. All investments carry a risk and in the trading of shares a key feature of investor protection is to ensure that accurate information is readily available so that potential investors can evaluate the risk involved.

2. The European Union has had a significant influence on legislation relating to public offer of shares, as free movement of capital within the EU depends upon efficient capital markets which in turn requires a harmonised system of regulation. The requirements relating to public offers of shares are now regulated by a series of EC Directives, the Public Offers of Securities Regulations 1995 and the Financial Services and Markets Act 2000, as well as the Stock Exchange Listing Rules.

3. The FSMA 2000 provides that the Financial Services Authority (FSA) is the United Kingdom's financial regulator. Under sections 1–6 FSMA 2000 its role is:
   ■ to maintain confidence in the financial system;
   ■ to promote public awareness in the financial system;
   ■ to protect consumers;
   ■ to reduce the extent to which financial services can be used for financial crime.

4. In order to be traded on an organised market, securities must be listed and every member state of the EU must have a Listing Authority, responsible for listing.

5. Under the Financial Services and Markets Act 2000, the Financial Services Authority is designated as the United Kingdom Listing Authority.

6. The United Kingdom Listing Authority (UKLA) maintains an Official List of those securities that are deemed suitable for trading on stock exchanges and are admitted to trading on at least one Recognised Investment Exchange (RIE). Of some 2.2 million registered companies in the United Kingdom, only about 2,700 are listed by the UKLA.

7. Listing is a separate process from admitting a company to trading on a stock exchange. A company that is admitted to official listing on a stock exchange must have completed both processes.

8. The London Stock Exchange operates a number of markets for the trading of securities: two of the most important are the Main Market, which is a 'regulated market' and is for listed companies, and the Alternative Investment Market (AIM), designed for younger, growing companies not admitted to the official list.

7.4.3 The regulatory framework: the prospectus and listing particulars

1. The principle underlying the regulation of public issues of shares is to ensure that investors are provided with full and accurate information about the issue.

2. Any company wishing to be traded on an organised market must go through the listing process. Under the Listing Particulars Directive (80/390 EEC), a company requiring listing must submit a set of listing particulars, which is a public document, to the UKLA. Detailed rules in relation to this are set out in the Listing Rules with additional provisions in the Financial Services and Markets Act 2000.

3. This is a separate process from admission to a regulated market and when a company applies for admission to a regulated market it must produce a prospectus.

4. A prospectus must also be made available to investors when a company (whether listed or not) proposes to offer shares to the public for the first time: Public Offers of Securities Regulations 1995.

5. The matters to be covered in the listing particulars and the prospectus are laid down in Chapters 5 and 6 of the Listing Rules.

6. Note that listing itself is a regulatory process, but the prospectus forms the basis of a contract for the sale of shares.

7. In general, the prospectus must disclose all the information which investors and their professional advisers would reasonably need in order to make an informed decision of whether to invest.

8. A prospectus must be approved by and filed with the FSA and made available to the public.

9. In July 2005 the New Prospectus Directive 2003/71/EC came into force. The purpose of the Directive is to improve regulation for raising capital on an EU-wide basis.

7.4.4 Remedies for misleading statements and omissions in listing particulars and prospectus

1. In relation to a prospectus or listing particulars, s 90 Financial Services and Markets Act 2000 provides that the person or persons responsible for any of the following is liable to pay compensation to a person who has acquired securities to which the particulars or prospectus apply for loss as a result of:

   ■ including a false or misleading statement in a prospectus or set of listing particulars;
   ■ failure to disclose information required to be included;
   ■ failure to publish a supplementary prospectus or set of listing particulars if required to do so.

2. Other remedies are also available to people induced to subscribe for shares by misleading or untrue statements under:

   ■ the common law, in both contract and tort;
   ■ Misrepresentation Act 1967;
   ■ Public Offers of Securities Regulations 1995, Regulations 13–15 if the misleading statement is in the prospectus.

3. It is a criminal offence to give false or misleading information in either the listing particulars or prospectus in connection with an application for a listing offer of shares to the public.

8

Maintenance of capital

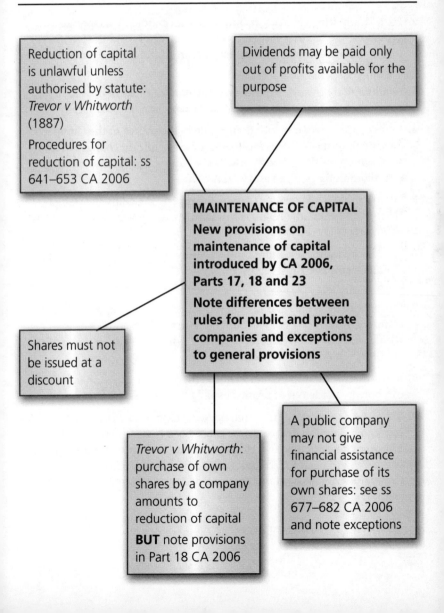

Reduction of capital is unlawful unless authorised by statute: *Trevor v Whitworth* (1887)

Procedures for reduction of capital: ss 641–653 CA 2006

Dividends may be paid only out of profits available for the purpose

MAINTENANCE OF CAPITAL

New provisions on maintenance of capital introduced by CA 2006, Parts 17, 18 and 23

Note differences between rules for public and private companies and exceptions to general provisions

Shares must not be issued at a discount

Trevor v Whitworth: purchase of own shares by a company amounts to reduction of capital

BUT note provisions in Part 18 CA 2006

A public company may not give financial assistance for purchase of its own shares: see ss 677–682 CA 2006 and note exceptions

8.1 General principles

1. The principle on which the rules relating to maintenance of capital are based is that a company should not pay share capital back to shareholders.

2. Historically the capital contribution of shareholders was intended to provide some security for the company's creditors and the law therefore lays down strict and complex rules in relation to the reduction of capital.

3. Share capital now often plays a relatively minor role in the financing of companies and the rules provide little protection for creditors.

4. In response to recommendations made in the course of the Company Law Review, the CA 2006 has made some significant changes in this area, which are described below. The statutory provisions are now contained in Parts 17, 18 and 23 CA 2006.

5. Share capital in this context means the money raised by the issue of shares and bears little relationship with the net worth of the company as a going concern.

6. There is no minimum share capital requirement for a private company; a public company must have a minimum share capital of at least £50,000.

7. Capital can be spent (and lost) in the course of carrying on the company's business, but it cannot be returned to members as this would amount to a reduction of capital with the result, in theory, that creditors would have less security.

8. In the case of a company not in liquidation, payments to shareholders can only be made out of profits, usually by way of dividend.

9. There are a number of rules that have developed to ensure that a company's capital, in the narrow sense used here, is maintained. These are described below. However, there are circumstances when a company will wish to reduce its capital and ss 641–653 of the Companies Act 2006 set out the procedures by which this may be done.

8.1.1 The main rules relating to the maintenance of capital

Relevant provision: CA 2006	General rule	Main exceptions
Part 17 Chapter 10	A company may not reduce its share capital: *Trevor v Whitworth* (1887)	A private company may reduce its capital by special resolution supported by solvency statement: s 641(a) Any company may reduce its share capital by special resolution confirmed by the court: s 641(b)
Part 23, s 831(1)	Distributions, including dividends may only be made out of profits available for the purpose	Except as provided for in Part 23
s 580(1)	Shares may not be allotted at a discount	
s 593	In the case of a public company, if shares are issued for a non-cash asset, the asset must be valued before allotment	
s 658	A limited company may not purchase its own shares except in accordance with Part 18	s 659 – purchase of own shares is not prohibited in a 'reduction of capital duly made'; in pursuance of an order of the court s 692 – a private company may purchase its own shares out of capital A public company may only purchase its own shares out of distributable profits

s 678	A public company may not give financial assistance for the purchase of its own shares	s 678 – it is not unlawful where the principal purpose in giving assistance is not for the acquisition of shares, but is for a larger purpose of the company, and the assistance is given in good faith in the interests of the company
s 677	Defines financial assistance	s 681 sets out certain transactions that do not amount to unlawful giving of financial assistance

8.2 Reduction of capital

8.2.1 The general rule

1. The general rule that a reduction of capital is unlawful unless authorised by statute was established in *Trevor v Whitworth* (1887).

2. The statutory provisions relating to reduction of capital are contained in ss 641–653 CA 2006. There are important differences in the provisions relating to private companies on the one hand and public companies on the other.

3. Under s 641:
   - any company may reduce its share capital by special resolution confirmed by the court: s 641(1)(b);
   - a private company limited by shares may reduce its share capital by passing a special resolution supported by a solvency statement: s 641(1)(a) and ss 642–644.

4. Thus, a private company may seek confirmation of the court but is no longer obliged to do so, while a public company can only reduce its capital with the authority of the court.

8.2.2 Private companies: the solvency statement

1. The solvency statement must be made not more than 15 days before the special resolution to reduce capital is passed.

2. Section 643 lays down requirements with respect to the solvency statement which must state *inter alia* that each of the directors is of the opinion that there is no ground on which the company could be found unable to pay its debts. If the directors make a solvency statement without having reasonable grounds for the opinion expressed, each director will be guilty of an offence.

3. The solvency statement, a statement of capital and the special resolution must be sent to the Registrar: s 644.

8.2.3 The role of the court

1. The court's main concern in approving reductions of capital is the protection of creditors, and the legislation provides opportunities for creditors to object (s 646).

2. In deciding whether to confirm a resolution for the reduction of capital the court must:
   - be assured that the interests of existing creditors are protected;
   - ensure that the procedure by which the reduction is carried out is correct (*Scottish Insurance Corporation Ltd v Wilsons & Clyde Coal Co Ltd* (1949)).

3. The court will not sanction a scheme if it is unfair. It must consider whether the scheme is fair and equitable between shareholders of different classes and between individual shareholders of the same class.

4. The court must be satisfied that the shareholders have received sufficient information to exercise an informed choice in voting on the special resolution.

8.3 Dividends

1. Distributions (which cover certain payments made to shareholders, including dividends) may be made only out of profits available for the purpose (s 830(1)). Procedures for this are laid down in Part 23 CA 2006. The Act lays down complex rules by which distributable profits are calculated.

2. Dividends may be declared as provided in the articles. Usually a declaration will be recommended by the directors and approved by the shareholders at the annual general meeting. Articles may also provide for an interim dividend to be declared by directors.

3. Members have a right to receive a dividend once it has been declared.

4. A public company cannot make a distribution which would result in the amount of the net assets becoming less than the aggregate of its called-up share capital and undistributable reserves (s 831(1)).

5. Directors who authorised an unlawful distribution may be liable to repay the money to the company.

6. Under s 847 a shareholder may be liable to repay an unlawful dividend if the shareholder knew or had reasonable grounds for believing that the distribution was made in contravention of Part 23.

8.4 Issues at a discount

1. Shares can be issued at below their market value, but members must pay at least the full nominal (or par) value for their shares. Section 580(1) provides that shares may not be allotted at a discount. (See also *Ooregum Gold Mining Co of India Ltd v Roper* (1892).) Section 580(2) CA 2006 provides in the event of contravention of this rule that the allottee must pay the amount of the discount plus interest.

2. If shares are paid for by a non-cash asset or assets, the rule may be difficult to enforce.

3. In the case of public companies, s 593 requires that if shares are issued for a consideration other than cash, the consideration must be valued before allotment. The section provides also that the valuer's report must be made to the company during the six months before the allotment and must be sent to the allottee.

4. In the case of private companies, there is no requirement that non-cash assets should be formally valued (*Re Wragg* (1897)).

8.5 Purchase by a company of its own shares

1. *Trevor v Whitworth* (1887) established the principle that a company may not purchase its own shares – this would amount to a reduction of capital.

2. This principle was inconvenient in a number of situations, especially for private companies, and some exceptions were introduced.

3. Section 658 CA 2006 now contains a provision to the effect that a limited company must not acquire its own shares except in accordance with the provisions in Part 18 of the Act. Part 18 lays down a complex set of rules enabling purchase by a company of its own shares. Section 658(2) provides that if a company acts in contravention of this section an offence is committed by the company and every officer in default and the purported acquisition is void.

4. Section 690 allows a limited company to purchase its own shares (including redeemable shares) subject to:
   - the provisions of Part 18 Chapter 4 of the Act, and
   - any restrictions in the company's articles.

5. In the case of public companies such purchases must be made out of distributable profits.

6. Private companies only may purchase their own shares out of capital, subject to any restriction in the articles and to safeguards for creditors (s 709).

7. A company can, subject to certain conditions, issue redeemable shares:
   - a public company can only issue redeemable shares if authorised by its articles;
   - a private company does not require authorisation by the articles, but the articles may limit or prohibit the issue of redeemable shares.

8. A public company can only redeem shares out of distributable profits or out of the proceeds of a fresh issue of shares made for the purpose of redemption. A private company may redeem shares out of capital.

9. Note: a company may not own shares in its holding company (s 136 CA 2006).

8.6 Financial assistance for purchase of own shares

8.6.1 CA 2006: the rules for public companies

1. The law in this area has been significantly changed by the Companies Act 2006. The general rule that a company may not give financial assistance for the purchase of its own shares has been abolished for private companies and applies now only to public companies.

2. Section 677 provides that unlawful financial assistance may occur when a company:
   - lends or gives money to someone to buy its shares;
   - lends or gives money to someone to pay back bank finance raised to buy its shares;
   - releases a debtor from liability to the company to assist the debtor to buy its shares;
   - guarantees or provides security for a bank loan to finance a purchase of its shares;
   - buys assets from a person at an overvalue to enable that person to purchase its shares (*Belmont Finance Corporation v Williams Furniture Ltd (No 2)* (1980)).

3. Section 678(1) provides that it is unlawful for a public company or its subsidiary to give financial assistance for the acquisition of shares in that company. The provision of such financial assistance is a criminal offence (s 680).

4. Under s 678(2) certain transactions are not unlawful. Financial assistance is not prohibited if:
   - it is given in good faith and in the interests of the company; and
   - the acquisition of shares is not the principal purpose, but is 'an incidental part of some larger purpose'.

   This section has caused great difficulty in practice and the House of Lords decision in *Brady v Brady* (1988) restricted its use.

5. In recent cases the courts have given effect to the 'commercial reality' of the situation and in a number of cases have found on that basis that financial assistance had not been given: for example, *MT Realisations Ltd v Digital Equipment Co Ltd* (2003); *Anglo Petroleum v TFB (Mortgages) Ltd* (2006); and see also *Chaston v SWP Group* (2002).

6. Under s 681 certain situations are not covered by the provisions above, including:
   - a distribution by way of a dividend or in the course of a winding up;
   - an allotment of bonus shares;
   - reduction of capital under Part 17 CA 2006;
   - anything done in the course of a compromise or arrangement under Part 26;
   - anything done under s 110 Insolvency Act 1986;
   - anything done under an arrangement between the company and its creditors under Part 1 Insolvency Act 1986.

7. Further exceptions, which apply subject to certain conditions, are set out in s 682. These include:
   - where the lending of money is part of the company's ordinary business and the money is lent in the ordinary course of business;
   - provision by the company of financial assistance for the purposes of an employees' share scheme;
   - loans to employees, other than directors, to enable them to acquire shares in the company or its holding company.

8.6.2 Remedies and sanctions

These are as follows:
   - a prohibited loan will be void;
   - the company and its officers may be fined;
   - directors may be liable to the company for misfeasance and breach of trust;
   - persons receiving funds who knew or ought to have known of the directors' breach of duty will be liable as constructive trustees (*Belmont Finance Corporation v Williams Furniture Ltd (No 2)* (1980)).

9

Company borrowing

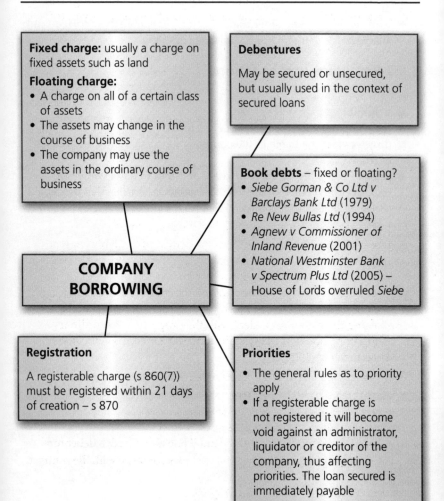

Fixed charge: usually a charge on fixed assets such as land

Floating charge:
- A charge on all of a certain class of assets
- The assets may change in the course of business
- The company may use the assets in the ordinary course of business

Debentures

May be secured or unsecured, but usually used in the context of secured loans

Book debts – fixed or floating?
- *Siebe Gorman & Co Ltd v Barclays Bank Ltd* (1979)
- *Re New Bullas Ltd* (1994)
- *Agnew v Commissioner of Inland Revenue* (2001)
- *National Westminster Bank v Spectrum Plus Ltd* (2005) – House of Lords overruled *Siebe*

COMPANY BORROWING

Registration

A registerable charge (s 860(7)) must be registered within 21 days of creation – s 870

Priorities
- The general rules as to priority apply
- If a registerable charge is not registered it will become void against an administrator, liquidator or creditor of the company, thus affecting priorities. The loan secured is immediately payable

9.1 Company charges

9.1.1 Debentures

1. It is very common for companies to raise capital by borrowing. This can take many forms, including bank overdrafts, promissory notes, mortgages on property and debentures. But note that a company's power to borrow may be limited by the articles of association.

2. The term 'debenture' has a very wide usage: it has been held to mean any document issued by a company acknowledging a debt (see for example *Lemon v Austin Friars Investment Trust Ltd* (1926)). It is defined in s 738 of the Companies Act 2006 (CA 2006): 'Debenture includes debenture stock, bonds and any other securities of a company, whether or not constituting a charge on the assets of the company'.

3. A debenture may be secured or unsecured. However, banks will usually require security for loans to companies and the term is generally used in the context of secured borrowing.

4. Security may be by means of a fixed or floating charge:
   ■ a **fixed charge** may be created over specified identifiable company property not dealt with by the company in its day-to-day business, for example its land and buildings;
   ■ a **floating charge** may be created over fluctuating assets, such as stock in trade, book debts, machinery, tools and other chattels, allowing the company to deal with the property in the ordinary course of business until crystallisation (*Re Yorkshire Woolcombers Association Ltd* (1903)).

5. There are significant differences between shares and debentures:
   ■ shares create rights of membership, for example the right to attend general meetings and vote; a debenture holder is a creditor of the company, whose rights are fixed by contract;
   ■ a shareholder is entitled to a dividend if one is declared; a debenture holder is entitled to payment of interest in accordance with the contract.

9.1.2 Fixed and floating charges

1. Whether a charge is fixed or floating is a matter of substance rather than form. Neither the words used by the parties nor their intentions will necessarily be conclusive in deciding how a charge

should be categorised (*Street v Mountford* (1985), *Re ASRS Establishment Ltd* (2000)). The distinction is important for a number of reasons:

■ In applying the principles relating to priority of payment, a fixed charge will generally take precedence over a floating charge.

■ Under provisions introduced by the Enterprise Act 2002, for charges created from 15 September 2003 a proportion of the assets of a company subject to a floating charge must be set aside for unsecured creditors. This is not the case with fixed charges, which makes fixed charges more attractive to banks and other chargees.

2. The main features indicating a floating charge have been expressed as:

■ it is a charge on all of a certain class of assets, present and future;

■ the assets may change in the ordinary course of business;

■ the company is able to carry on its business using the assets in the ordinary way (*Re Yorkshire Woolcombers Association Ltd* (1903)).

9.1.3 Book debts

1. Cases involving book debts have raised a number of issues in relation to the distinction between fixed and floating charges. Until the House of Lords decision in *Re Spectrum Plus Ltd* (2005) there had been some confusion as to how book debts and their proceeds should be treated.

2. In *Re Brightlife Ltd* (1987) the company was not restricted from dealing with either the debts or the proceeds and it was held that this arrangement created a floating charge.

3. More difficult situations arise in cases where there are restrictions on assigning the book debts, but the company has freedom to draw on the account into which the proceeds of the debts are deposited. This was the case in *Siebe Gorman & Co Ltd v Barclays Bank Ltd* (1979): there were restrictions on the company's use of its book debts and the proceeds were paid into an account held by the lender, although the company was free to draw on the account. It was held that this arrangement created a fixed charge. This case was followed, and relied upon by banks, until it was overruled by *Re Spectrum Plus Ltd* (2005).

4. In *Re New Bullas Ltd* (1994) while the book debts were expressed as a fixed charge, the proceeds were released from the charge and paid into a bank account controlled by the company. It was held that a distinction could be made between the book debts, which were subject to a fixed charge, and the proceeds, subject to a floating charge.

5. The Privy Council case *Agnew v Commissioner of Inland Revenue* (2001) clarified the law in this area. In this case a charge similar to that in *New Bullas* had been created in favour of a bank. The court held that *New Bullas* had been wrongly decided and expressed the opinion that separating the debt from the proceeds 'made no commercial sense'. Lord Millett set out a two-stage process for categorising fixed and floating charges:
   - first the court must consider the intention of the parties as to their respective rights and obligations;
   - the second stage requires the court to determine whether the charge is fixed or floating as a matter of law.

   In *Agnew* the company was able to realise the debt and to pay the proceeds into an account which it controlled. This was held to be a floating charge.

6. In *Re Spectrum Plus Ltd* (2005) the proceeds of the debts were paid into a current account held by the bank but the company was able to draw on the account and make use of the overdraft facility, so this could not be a fixed charge. The commercial reality of the situation must be taken into account. *Siebe* and *Re New Bullas Ltd* were overruled, resolving many of the uncertainties in the law.

9.1.4 Crystallisation

1. A floating charge crystallises and becomes fixed on the occurrence of certain events. The chargee takes possession or appoints an administrator or receiver.

2. A floating charge crystallises:
   - on cessation of the company's business (*Re Woodroffes (Musical Instruments) Ltd* (1986));
   - when the security is enforced by virtue of a clause in the debenture (*Re Brightlife Ltd* (1986));
   - when the company goes into administration or receivership;
   - when the company goes into liquidation.

9.2 Registration and priorities

9.2.1 Legal and equitable charges

1. A charge may be legal or equitable:
   - a legal charge must be recognised by anyone who gains title to the charged property after the charge is created;
   - an equitable charge must be recognised by anyone other than a person who acquires the property *bona fide* and for value, without notice (actual or constructive) of the charge.

9.2.2 Effect of registration

1. A charge must be registered at Companies House in accordance with s 860 CA 2006. Section 870 provides that a registerable charge, as listed in s 860(7), must be registered within 21 days of its creation. Registration provides actual notice of the charge to anyone who consults the register and constructive notice to others (*Wilson v Lelland* (1910)). The register is open to public inspection. The requirement of registration ensures that a subsequent creditor seeking security by way of a floating charge (which is an equitable charge) has either actual or constructive notice of any existing charges on the property.

2. Failure to register a charge may result in the company and its officers being fined.

9.2.3 Priorities

1. Charges created by a company are subject to the general rules governing priority.

2. A legal charge will rank in priority over an equitable charge. Thus a legal mortgage will rank in priority before a floating charge, even if the mortgage was created after the floating charge.

3. Between two floating charges the order of creation will determine priority, with the charge created first ranking ahead of the second, unless there is an express provision in the first charge that the company may create a second charge taking priority: *Re Automatic Bottlemakers Ltd* (1926).

4. Registration affects priority. If a charge is not registered within the required 21 days it will lose all priority.

5. Under s 874, if a registerable charge is not registered, it will be void against an administrator of the company, a liquidator of the company and a creditor of the company. When a charge becomes void under this section, the money secured by it immediately becomes payable (s 874(3)), but it will no longer be treated as a secured debt.

9.2.4 Reform

1. The current law on registration of charges, as set out in the CA 2006, has been the subject of criticism for some time and a consultation on the registration of charges created by companies and limited liability partnerships was issued in May 2010.

2. The consultation makes proposals to revise the current law and is based on recommendations made in 2001 in the course of the Company Law Review and on advice of the Law Commission. Consideration is given to:
   - which charges must be registered;
   - how charges may be registered including the possibility of electronic registration;
   - the consequences of registering or not registering a registerable charge.

3. It is intended to publish draft regulations in 2011 and change is likely to be implemented in 2012 or 2013.

10

Corporate governance

Accountability of company directors
- The role of shareholders
- Auditors
- Non-executive directors

'COMPLY OR EXPLAIN'

The UK Corporate Governance Code
- Leadership
- Effectiveness
- Accountability
- Remuneration
- Dialogue with shareholders

10.1 Introduction

1. As described in chapter 3, a company is a separate legal person, able to conduct business. However, a company can only act through agents and, apart from small, owner-managed companies (quasi-partnerships), it is usual for shareholders to delegate management of the company to directors, who may or may not also be members of the company.

2. Company directors have extensive powers of management and shareholders need to be confident that a framework exists to restrict the ability of managers to abuse those powers. This chapter will note, with reference to the chapters that follow, those areas where shareholders themselves can control the conduct of directors and will briefly describe the system of regulation developed over the last two decades, culminating in the UK Corporate Governance Code.

3. It is important to bear in mind when considering corporate governance that there are big differences between large companies where the power to manage the company is delegated to directors on the one hand and quasi-partnerships where the shareholders are also the directors on the other.

10.2 Accountability of directors: issues and responses

1. In any company it will be in the shareholders' interest that the directors have the authority to develop strategies and make decisions to promote the success of the company, and there is a balance to be struck between allowing the directors the freedom to manage the company and ensuring that they do so in the company's best interest rather than their own. The Companies Act 2006 reserves certain rights to shareholders, but it has become apparent in recent years that there is a need for separate regulation, developed through a series of self-regulatory codes.

2. Corporate governance is about how companies are structured and regulated to ensure that those in control operate in such a way as to promote the long-term success of the company for the benefit of shareholders and other stakeholders. The sections that follow describe the relationship of the shareholders and the board of directors, internal mechanisms for control and the development of regulatory codes.

10.2.1 Shareholders and the board of directors

1. Corporate governance in the UK is centred on shareholders. There has been growing criticism of this approach as being too focused on shareholders to the exclusion of other stakeholders. Section 172 CA 2006 now requires directors to consider the interests of others, including employees, in the exercise of their duties; but as there is no direct way of enforcing these duties, this is not likely to make very much difference.

2. The balance of power between shareholders in general meeting and the board of directors is determined by the Companies Act 2006 and the articles of association (see chapter 11). The articles of association will usually delegate powers of management to the directors, but these may be qualified, for example there may be a provision requiring approval by the general meeting for certain acts.

3. The articles usually provide for election of directors by the general meeting and CA 2006 s 168 provides that shareholders may by ordinary resolution remove directors. However, because individual shareholders are widely dispersed in large companies and have relatively small holdings they are more likely to sell their shares if they are dissatisfied than to seek to remove directors.

4. Directors have certain duties, now contained in ss 171–178 CA 2006. Note particularly s 172, which requires directors to 'promote the success of the company'. However, these duties are owed to the company not to individual shareholders (see chapter 12).

5. Under the rule in *Foss v Harbottle*, if a wrong is done to the company, it is the company that has the right of action against the wrongdoer. The right to litigate is usually exercised by the board of directors, which causes difficulty if the wrongdoers are the directors themselves. CA 2006 s 260 provides that in certain circumstances a shareholder may bring a derivative claim against directors of the company. This is a new statutory provision and the extent to which it will be used is not yet known, but there are still significant barriers to the exercise of this right (see chapter 14).

6. In large public companies individual shareholders with relatively small holdings will not have any real influence on the management of the company. However, the increasing influence of institutional investors such as insurance companies and pension funds does have an impact, although not necessarily through voting in general meetings.

7. It can be seen that the power of shareholders to influence the conduct of directors is often theoretic rather than real in large companies where power to manage it is delegated.

10.2.2 Auditors

Unless they are exempt for reasons set out in the Companies Act 2006, companies are required to appoint auditors, who may be appointed by either the members or the directors. The role of the auditors is to ensure that the directors provide a 'true and fair view' of the company's financial state. The auditors' report must be sent to all members of a private company (under the 2006 Act, private companies are not required to hold annual general meetings) and must be presented to the annual general meeting of a public company.

10.2.3 Regulation

1. High profile examples of corporate mismanagement (for example, *BCCI*, *Maxwell*, *Enron*) reinforced the need for a framework of regulation which sets out principles of corporate governance.
2. This has been recommended by various reports:
   - In 1992 the Cadbury Committee published its *Report on the Financial Aspects of Corporate Governance.* In this report corporate governance was defined as 'the system by which companies are directed and controlled'.
   - This was followed in 1995 by the Greenbury *Report on Directors' Remuneration.*
   - In 1998 the Hampel Committee published its *Final Report* and, in consultation with the Stock Exchange, produced the *Combined Code* which contained principles of good governance and a code of good practice.
   - The Higgs *Report on Non-Executive Directors* was published in January 2003 and at the same time the Financial Reporting Council released new guidance for audit committees.
   - A revised version of the *Combined Code* was published in June 2006.
3. The UK Corporate Governance Code was published in June 2010 following review by the Financial Reporting Council. It applies to listed companies, but all companies are encouraged to have regard to the Code. This, like the combined code, does not have the force of legislation, but rather it is a framework for self-regulation (*Re Astec (BSR) plc* (1999)).

10.3 The UK Corporate Governance Code

10.3.1 Principles

In the introduction to the Code it is stated that the purpose of corporate governance is 'to facilitate effective, entrepreneurial and prudent management that can deliver the long-term success of the company'. The Code contains a number of principles under five sections, each of which contains supporting principles and more specific code provisions. The main principles may be summarised as follows:

1. *Section A: Leadership.* Every listed company should be headed by an effective board which provides entrepreneurial leadership; there should be a clear division of responsibility between the Chairman and Chief Executive and the board should include a balance of executive and non-executive directors, so that no individual or group of individuals can dominate the board's decision-making.

2. *Section B: Effectiveness.* This section is concerned with matters such as the appropriate balance of skills and experience on the board of directors, transparent procedures for appointment of new directors on the board, induction of new directors and the requirement for formal evaluation of its own performance annually. The Code sets out guidelines for the proportion of non-executive directors, who must be independent of the management of the company and who have a monitoring and strategic role on the board.

3. *Section C: Accountability.* It is the board's responsibility to present a balanced and understandable assessment of the company's position and prospects; effective controls should be in place to manage risks and the board is responsible for determining the extent of the risks it is willing to take to enable the company to meet its strategic objectives. Auditors play a key role in ensuring accountability for financial matters.

4. *Section D: Remuneration.* Levels of remuneration should be sufficient to attract, retain and motivate the directors needed to run the company successfully, but companies should avoid paying more than necessary; there should be a formal and transparent procedure for developing policy on executive remuneration and for fixing individual remuneration and no director should be involved in deciding his or her own remuneration.

5. *Section E: Relations with shareholders.* The board is responsible for ensuring that there is a satisfactory dialogue with shareholders and should use the AGM to communicate with shareholders and encourage shareholder participation.

10.3.2 'Comply or explain'

1. Companies have been required to disclose certain matters since 1844. The Companies Act 2006 requires that certain information is given to shareholders, for example, company accounts. The Code also requires listed companies to provide information about how and to what extent they comply with the principles of the Code.

2. The principle of 'comply or explain' has been in operation from the first corporate governance Code. It is an important feature of UK corporate governance, giving it a degree of flexibility. It is recognised that different companies have different needs and that good governance can be achieved in different ways. The Code is a statement of good practice but there may be circumstances where governance is achieved by other means. Thus if a company does not comply with the Code it is required to explain to shareholders in its Annual Report how its own actual practices are consistent with the principles of the Code and contribute to good governance.

11

Directors

Appointment

- first directors appointed by subscribers to memorandum
- subsequent appointment in accordance with company's articles of association
- s 157 – a director must be at least 16 years of age

May be subject to disqualification

- Company Directors Disqualification Act 1986
- undischarged bankrupts

Termination of office

- retirement – by rotation
- resignation
- removal from office: s 168

DIRECTORS

Contracts of service

- directors are not automatically employees
- terms of contract must be available for inspection by members: s 228
- terms of office longer than two years need approval from members: s 188

Division of power between general meeting and board of directors

- Powers of management are usually delegated to the board of directors: Art 3 Draft Model Articles for both public companies and private companies limited by shares
- In such cases the general meeting has no power by ordinary resolution to give directions to the board or overrule its decisions
- Companies Act 2006 and Insolvency Act 1986 reserve certain powers to the general meeting
- Shareholders in general meeting may act if there is no competent board: *Barron v Potter* (1914)

11.1 Introduction

1. A company is an artificial person and as such can only act through agents.

2. Under s 154 of the Companies Act 2006 (CA 2006) every private company must have at least one director and a public company must have two. Every company must have at least one director that is a natural person.

3. There is no definition of a director, but s 250 CA 2006 provides that 'director' means any person carrying out the role of director, by whatever term described, and includes a 'shadow director'.

4. A shadow director is 'a person in accordance with whose directions or instructions the directors of a company are accustomed to act' (s 251(1) CA 2006).

5. The Act does not require companies to be managed by the directors, but Art 3 of the model articles for both public companies and private companies limited by shares provide that 'subject to the articles, the directors are responsible for the management of the company's business, for which purpose they may exercise all the powers of the company'.

6. Every company must keep a register of directors and, where relevant, company secretary at its registered office and must notify the Registrar of Companies of any changes within 14 days.

11.2 Appointment

1. Provisions relating to the appointment of directors, maximum and minimum numbers, quoracy, whether the chairman has a casting vote, and similar matters will be included in the company's articles of association.

2. CA 2006 introduced a new minimum age provision. Under s 157 a director must be at least 16 years of age on taking office. Under s 159 any existing director under 16 ceased to be a director when s 157 came into force.

11.2.1 Who appoints directors?

1. Under s 9(4)(c) CA 2006 the first directors are appointed by a statement in the prescribed form signed by the subscribers to the memorandum. The statement must also be signed by the directors to show that they consent to act in that capacity (s 12(3)).

2. Subsequent directors are appointed by members by ordinary resolution (*Woolf v East Nigel Gold Mining Co Ltd* (1905)).

3. Section 160 provides that in the case of a public company every director must be voted on individually unless it is agreed at the meeting, without anyone voting against the resolution, that the vote should be composite.

4. A company's articles of association may contain provisions for the appointment of directors. The model articles for private companies limited by shares (Art 17(1)) and public companies (Art 20) provide that directors may be appointed:
   - by ordinary resolution, or
   - by decision of the directors.

11.2.2 Defective appointment and disqualification

1. Section 161 provides that the acts of a director are valid even if there is a defect in his or her appointment or qualification. However, this section does not apply when there has been no appointment at all (*Morris v Kanssen* (1946)).

2. Certain persons may be disqualified from acting as directors:
   - anyone who is the subject of a disqualification order under the Company Directors Disqualification Act 1986;
   - it is an offence of strict liability, triable either way, for an undischarged bankrupt to act as a director without the leave of the court (*R v Brockley* (1994));
   - a sole director cannot also be the company secretary.

11.3 Termination of office

11.3.1 Retirement and resignation

1. Model articles for public companies, Art 21 provides:
   - all directors must retire at the first AGM, but may seek reappointment;

- one third of directors must retire by rotation each year, but may seek reappointment.

2. A director may resign by giving notice to the company which the company must accept. The articles may stipulate certain requirements, for example that notice must be in writing.

11.3.2 Removal from office

1. Directors (either individually or as a board) may be removed by the shareholders by ordinary resolution (s 168 CA 2006).

2. Conditions for removal are that:
   - special notice must be given of a resolution to remove directors (s 168(2));
   - a copy must be supplied to the director who is the subject of the resolution;
   - note that in any company a resolution to remove a director before his term ends must be taken at a meeting;
   - the director is entitled to make representations in writing (which must be circulated to every member) and he is entitled to be heard at the meeting;
   - removal under s 168 does not deprive the director of any claim for compensation or damages payable in respect of loss of office.

3. The shareholders' right to remove directors as set out in s 168 applies notwithstanding any provision to the contrary in the company's constitution, but see *Bushell v Faith* (1969) where the House of Lords held that a weighted voting rights clause, which effectively prevented the removal of a director in a small private company, was valid.

4. Removal of a director under s 168 may incur liability for breach of any contract of service which may exist between the company and the director (*Southern Foundries v Shirlaw* (1940); *Shindler v Northern Raincoat Co Ltd* (1960); *Read v Astoria Garage (Sreatham) Ltd* (1952)).

5. In certain circumstances, especially in small closely-held companies, s 122(1)(g) Insolvency Act 1986 and s 994 CA 2006 have been used by directors threatened with removal: *Harman v BML Group Ltd* (1994); *Re Bird Precision Bellows Ltd* (1986) and see chapter 14.

11.4 Remuneration

1. Directors are not entitled to remuneration unless provided for in the constitution (*Hutton v West Cork Railway Co* (1883)).

2. Provision is usually made in the articles to pay directors: model articles for private companies limited by shares Art 19, and for public companies Art 23.

11.5 Directors as employees

1. Directors are not automatically employees of their companies. A director (especially an executive director) may have a separate contract of service with the company.

2. Whether a director is an employee or not is a question of fact (*Secretary of State for Trade and Industry v Bottrill* (1999)).

3. A copy of every director's service contract or a memorandum setting out the terms of the contract of service must be available for inspection by members (s 228).

4. A term in a director's contract which provides that the director shall be employed for more than two years which cannot be terminated by notice by the company must be approved by resolution of the members (s 188).

11.6 Division of power between general meeting and the board

11.6.1 General power of management

1. Companies will usually delegate powers of management to the board of directors. The extent of such powers is determined by the relevant articles in the articles of association.

2. Where the general management of the company is vested in the directors (as in Art 3 model articles for both private and public companies), the shareholders have no power by ordinary resolution to give directions to the Board or overrule their business decisions (*Automatic Self-Cleansing Filter Syndicate Co Ltd v Cuninghame* (1906); *John Shaw & Sons (Salford) Ltd v Shaw* (1935)).

3. The right to litigate on behalf of the company is an aspect of management and as such is also vested in the board of directors (*Breckland Group Holdings v London & Suffolk Properties Ltd* (1989)). This can cause difficulty where the directors themselves have committed a wrong against the company.

4. Article 70 Table A Company Act 1985 states: 'Subject to the provisions of the Act, the memorandum and the articles and to any directions given by special resolution, the business of the company shall be managed by the directors who may exercise all the powers of the Company'. Article 70 also provides that no such direction shall invalidate any prior action of the directors.

5. The Companies Act 2006 model articles for both private companies limited by shares and public companies contain provisions similar in effect but more clearly expressed:
   - Art 3: subject to the articles, the directors are responsible for the management of the company's business, for which purposes they may exercise all the powers of the company.
   - Art 4(1): the members may, by special resolution, direct the directors to take, or refrain from taking, specified action.
   - Art 4(2): no such special resolution invalidates anything which the directors have already done.

6. The courts have taken a restrictive view of the power of members to direct the board and the members' reserve power contained in Art 4 of the model articles appears to be limited to specific instances rather than a general power to direct the board.

7. A company may restrict the powers of directors by provision in the articles. For example in *Salmon, Quin v Axtens* (1909) the articles gave a general power of management to the board of directors, but also gave a veto to one of two named directors on certain matters. It was held by the Court of Appeal (affirmed by the House of Lords) that the veto should be upheld and an ordinary resolution that sought to override it was ineffective.

8. A large number of powers are reserved to the general meeting by the Companies Act 2006 and the Insolvency Act 1986.

11.6.2 Default powers of the general meeting

1. The general meeting may ratify an act of the directors which is voidable as an irregular exercise of their powers (*Bamford v Bamford* (1970)).

2. The company in general meeting may act if there is no board competent or able to exercise the powers conferred on it (*Baron v Potter* (1914)).

11.6.3 Power and accountability

Directors have great powers. Chapter 10 and this chapter have dealt with some of these powers and some of the rules and principles of company law and corporate governance regulation designed to ensure that directors are accountable for their actions. The following chapters continue this theme in the context of directors' duties, shareholder remedies, takeovers and mergers and insolvency procedures.

12

Directors' duties

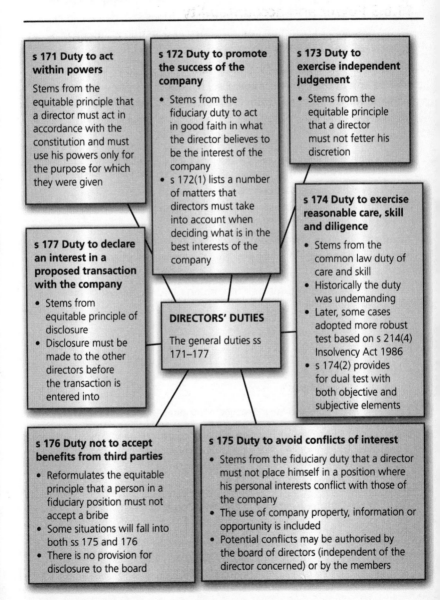

s 171 Duty to act within powers

Stems from the equitable principle that a director must act in accordance with the constitution and must use his powers only for the purpose for which they were given

s 172 Duty to promote the success of the company

- Stems from the fiduciary duty to act in good faith in what the director believes to be the interest of the company
- s 172(1) lists a number of matters that directors must take into account when deciding what is in the best interests of the company

s 173 Duty to exercise independent judgement

- Stems from the equitable principle that a director must not fetter his discretion

s 177 Duty to declare an interest in a proposed transaction with the company

- Stems from equitable principle of disclosure
- Disclosure must be made to the other directors before the transaction is entered into

DIRECTORS' DUTIES

The general duties ss 171–177

s 174 Duty to exercise reasonable care, skill and diligence

- Stems from the common law duty of care and skill
- Historically the duty was undemanding
- Later, some cases adopted more robust test based on s 214(4) Insolvency Act 1986
- s 174(2) provides for dual test with both objective and subjective elements

s 176 Duty not to accept benefits from third parties

- Reformulates the equitable principle that a person in a fiduciary position must not accept a bribe
- Some situations will fall into both ss 175 and 176
- There is no provision for disclosure to the board

s 175 Duty to avoid conflicts of interest

- Stems from the fiduciary duty that a director must not place himself in a position where his personal interests conflict with those of the company
- The use of company property, information or opportunity is included
- Potential conflicts may be authorised by the board of directors (independent of the director concerned) or by the members

12.1 Introduction

1. One of the most significant changes made by the Companies Act 2006 (CA 2006) is the codification of the duties owed to a company by its directors. Previously, the law on directors' duties was perceived as a complex web of common law, fiduciary and statutory rules and principles, some of which overlapped and which were sometimes not entirely consistent with one another.

2. The reform of the law was the subject of extensive review and consultation by the Law Commission and the Company Law Review Steering Group.

3. The general duties of directors are set out in Part 10, Chapter 2 CA 2006. In *Modern Company Law for a Competitive Economy: Final Report*, a legislative statement of directors' duties was recommended in order to:
   - achieve clarity and accessibility of the law;
   - correct perceived defects in the law, particularly relating to conflicts of interest;
   - address the question of the 'scope' of directors' duties.

4. The Act sets out seven general duties in ss 171–177. These are based on the equitable principles arising from the fiduciary relationship between a director and his or her company and on the common law of negligence.

s 171	Duty to act within powers
s 172	Duty to promote the success of the company for the benefit of its members as a whole
s 173	Duty to exercise independent judgement
s 174	Duty to exercise reasonable care, skill and diligence
s 175	Duty to avoid conflicts of interest
s 176	Duty not to accept benefits from third parties
S 177	Duty to declare any interest in proposed transactions

5. It is well established that directors owe duties to the company, not to individual shareholders or to shareholders collectively (*Percival v Wright* (1902); *Peskin v Anderson* (2000)). The Act now provides, under

s 170(1), that 'The general duties specified in sections 171 to 177 are owed by a director of a company to the company'. It follows that these duties can be enforced by the company only but note the new statutory derivative claim in Part 11 CA 2006: see Chapter 14 below.

6. Because of their position, directors owe a duty of loyalty to their company and it is this duty that underpins the fiduciary duties set out in the Act. These duties are owed by directors and *de facto* directors. A *de facto* director is a person who assumes the role of director and is held out as a director, but has never actually been appointed. It is not clear whether shadow directors owe a duty of loyalty to the company *(Ultraframe (UK) v Fielding* (2005)) and it is likely that the courts will decide each case on its own facts.

7. Section 178 provides that the consequences of breach of the general duties set out in ss 171–177 are the same as would apply if the corresponding common law rule or equitable principle applied.

8. The statutory duties of disclosure previously contained in Part X CA 1985 have been re-enacted in Part 10 Chapter 4 CA 2006.

12.2 The general duties

1. Section 170(4) CA 2006 provides: 'The general duties shall be interpreted and applied in the same way as common law rules or equitable principles, and regard shall be had to the corresponding common law rules and equitable principles in interpreting and applying the general duties'. Thus the case law developed prior to the CA 2006 continues to be relevant.

2. This is intended to strike a balance between predictability of statute and the ability of the courts to develop principles through the doctrine of judicial precedent.

12.2.1 Duty to act within powers

1. Directors must act in accordance with the company's constitution and must only exercise their powers for purposes for which they are conferred: s 171.

2. The articles of association may limit the powers of directors. If a company has restricted objects its directors must not act outside those objects.

3. If powers are given to directors for a particular purpose they must not be used for some other purpose and directors must not use their powers to further their own personal interests (*Lee Panavision Ltd v Lee Lighting Ltd* (1992)).

4. A misuse of power will be a breach of duty even if the directors are acting in what they believe to be the best interests of the company.

5. A number of cases involve the allotment of shares. It is a breach of duty to allot shares to avoid a takeover (*Hogg v Cramphorn Ltd* (1967)) or to alter the weight of shareholder votes to influence the outcome of a takeover bid (*Howard Smith Ltd v Ampol Petroleum Ltd* (1974)).

6. It will sometimes be arguable that the act in question was carried out to achieve more than one purpose, only one of which may be a misuse of power. For example, in *Howard Smith Ltd v Ampol Petroleum Ltd* shares were allotted not only to alter the balance of voting power to avoid a takeover, but also to raise capital (a valid reason for the allotment of shares). In this kind of situation the courts will decide whether the improper purpose was the main or dominant purpose. In this case it was held that it was and the directors were in breach of their duty.

7. Acts in breach of the proper purpose rule can be ratified by shareholders (*Bamford v Bamford* (1970)).

12.2.2 Duty to promote the success of the company

1. This stems from the equitable principle that directors must act *bona fide* in what they consider to be the best interests of the company as a whole (*Re Smith & Fawcett Ltd* (1942) and see *Item Software (UK) Ltd v Fassihi* (2004)).

2. Section 172(1) provides: 'A director of a company must act in the way he considers, in good faith, would be most likely to promote the success of the company for the benefit of its members as a whole . . . '.

3. The duty is subjective. The question is whether the directors honestly believed that their act or omission was in the best interest of the company at the time the decision was made. The court will not seek to make its own commercial judgment but will consider all the evidence to determine what the directors believed (see *Regentcrest v Cohen* (2001); *Item Software (UK) Ltd v Fassihi* (2004)).

4. Whether directors should consider wider constituencies (or stakeholders) than the company and its shareholders in managing the

company has long been a question for discussion by commentators.
Now s 172(1) lists a number of matters that the directors must consider
in making decisions:

(a) the likely consequences of the decision in the long term;
(b) the interests of the company's employees;
(c) the need to foster the company's business relationships with
    suppliers, customers and others;
(d) the impact of the company's operations on the community and the
    environment;
(e) the desirability of the company maintaining a reputation for high
    standards of business conduct;
(f) the need to act fairly as between members of the company.

5. The section makes it clear that directors must act not only in the
   interests of the company as a separate entity, but must consider also
   the benefit of its members as a body. Furthermore, the list above is
   intended to ensure that the interests of other factors are taken into
   account as well in the board's decision-making.

6. Section 172(1)(b) replaces s 309 CA 1985, which provided that the
   directors must have regard to 'the interests of the Company's employees in general as well as the interests of members'.

7. Creditors are not specifically included above. However, s 172(3)
   provides that the duty imposed by s 172 is subject to any enactment or
   rule of law to consider the interests of creditors in certain
   circumstances. In general, directors do not owe duties to the company's
   creditors, but if a company is insolvent it has been held that directors
   must have regard to the interest of creditors (*West Mercia Safetywear Ltd
   v Dodd* (1988); *Colin Gwyer and Associates Ltd v London Wharf (Limehouse)
   Ltd* (2002)).

12.2.3 Duty to exercise independent judgement

1. Section 173 provides that directors have a duty to exercise independent
   judgement and not to fetter their discretion. This may be considered
   part of their general duty to act *bona fida* and to promote the success
   of the company. However, it is well established that directors must
   not bind themselves to act in a particular way regardless of whether
   it would be in the best interests of the company. However, it is not a
   breach of duty for directors to enter into a binding contract which may
   have the effect of fettering their discretion at a later date, if they believe
   the agreement to be in the best interests of the company at the time that

the agreement is made (*Fulham Football Club v Cabra Estates plc* (1994); *Dawsons International plc v Coats Patons plc* (1989)).

2. Another situation where the duty to exercise independent judgement might arise is where a director is nominated by an 'outsider' for example by a holding company to sit on the board of a subsidiary. In such cases it has been held that the primary duty of the nominee is to the company of which he is a director, but that he may take account of the interests of the 'outsider' as long as this is not incompatible with his primary duty: *Re Neath Rugby Ltd* (2008).

12.2.4 Duty to exercise reasonable care, skill and diligence

1. Directors owe a duty of competence to the company, but historically the standard of care expected of them has been undemanding (*Re Brazilian Rubber Plantations and Estates Ltd* (1911)). Reasons for this approach included:

   - directors were sometimes appointed more because of their social standing than because they had particular skills or qualifications;
   - the courts did not wish to deter people from becoming company directors by imposing onerous duties of care and skill.

2. This duty was categorised into three propositions by Romer J in *Re City Equitable Fire Insurance Co* (1925):

   (a) A director was expected to show a degree of care and skill as may reasonably be expected from a person of his/her knowledge and experience. Note that the standard of care test was expressed in subjective terms, so a director was only expected to act with the degree of care and skill which he or she happened to possess and was not expected to have any particular qualifications or any experience of the company's area of business.

   (b) A director is not bound to give continuous attention to the affairs of the company (*Re Cardiff Savings Bank* (1892)).

   (c) Subject to normal business practice, directors may leave routine conduct of business affairs in the hands of management.

3. In later cases the courts have adopted a more robust approach (*Dorchester Finance v Stebbing* (1989); *Norman v Theodore Goddard* (1991); *Re d'Jan of London Ltd* (1994); *Re Simmon Box (Diamonds) Ltd* (2000) and *Base Metal Trading Ltd v Shamurin* (2004)).

4. The test that was applied in these more recent cases had an objective element, based on s 214(4) Insolvency Act 1986:
   - the general knowledge, skill and experience that may reasonably be expected of a person carrying out the same functions as are carried out by that director in relation to the company, and
   - the general knowledge, skill and experience that that director has.

5. In *Barings plc (No 5)* (2000) negligence on the part of company directors was considered in the context of an application for disqualification under the Company Directors Disqualification Act 1986. It was held that:
   - directors have an obligation to acquire enough knowledge and understanding of the company's business to enable them to discharge their duties properly;
   - they may, subject to any restriction in the articles, delegate certain functions to others, but this does not absolve them from a duty to exercise proper supervision (see also *Re Queens Moat House plc (No 2)* (2005));
   - the extent of this duty will depend on the facts of the particular case.

6. Development of the law has been influenced by a number of factors including:
   (a) There is an expectation of a more professional approach to company directorship than existed in the first half of the twentieth century, for example directors should pay proper attention to the management of the company and if as part of the role they have a duty to perform a particular action they will be in breach for failing to do so: *Lexi Holdings Ltd plc v Luqman* (2009). However, a director who takes and acts upon appropriate legal advice will not be negligent: *Green v Walkling* (2007).
   (b) It is usual now to appoint appropriately qualified people to designated executive directorships, for example finance director.
   (c) Contracts of service for executive directors may contain clauses relating to care and skill, which may help to define the scope of the director's duty of care and skill.

7. However, it must be recognised that investing in a company carries some risk, managers may not be of the highest calibre and not every error of judgement will amount to negligence: *Re Elgindata Ltd* (1991).

8. Section 174 codifies the law by providing that a company director must exercise reasonable care, skill and diligence.

- Under s 174(2) the dual test, as set out in s 214 IA 1986, with both objective and subjective elements must be applied in deciding whether a director is in breach of this duty.
- The standard of care, skill and diligence is defined as that which would be exercised by a reasonably diligent person with:
  - (a) 'the general knowledge, skill and experience that may reasonably be expected of a person carrying out the functions carried out by the director in relation to the company, and
  - (b) the general knowledge, skill and experience that the director has'.

12.2.5 Duty to avoid conflicts of interest

1. Directors owe a duty of loyalty to their company: see *Item Software (UK) Ltd v Fassihi* (2004) where Arden LJ emphasised the 'fundamental nature of the duty of loyalty'.

2. Section 175(1) CA 2006 provides: 'A director of a company must avoid a situation in which he has, or can have, a direct or indirect interest that conflicts, or possibly may conflict, with the interests of the company'. The duty does not apply to a conflict arising from a transaction or arrangement with the company itself (s 175(3)).

3. The section is a statutory statement of the well established equitable principle stated in *Aberdeen Railway Company v Blaikie Bros* (1854): 'it is a rule of universal application that no one, having such (fiduciary) duties to discharge, shall be allowed to enter into engagements in which he has, or can have, a personal interest conflicting, or which possibly may conflict, with the interests of those whom he is bound to protect'.

4. Section 175(2) brings the exploitation of any property, information or opportunity within the section and makes it clear that it is immaterial whether or not the company could take advantage of the property, information or opportunity.

5. A number of cases deal with exploitation by a director of a corporate opportunity. A corporate opportunity is regarded as a corporate asset, which directors may not use for their own benefit. This applies even if it would be impossible for the company itself to make use of the opportunity (*Industrial Development Consultants Ltd v Cooley* (1972)).

6. Furthermore, a director may still be in breach of fiduciary duties in circumstances where he or she resigns to take up the opportunity: *CMS Dolphin Ltd v Simonet* (2001); *Bhullar v Bhullar* (2003); *Foster Bryant*

Surveying Ltd v Bryant (2007). In *Bhullar* Jonathan Parker LJ said that the no-profit and no-conflict rules are universal and inflexible, and s 170(2)(a) now provides that a person who ceases to be a director continues to be subject 'to the duty in s 175 (duty to avoid conflicts of interest) as regards the exploitation of any property, information or opportunity of which he became aware at the time when he was a director'.

7. However, much will depend on the nature of the corporate opportunity and the timing of taking it up, for example in *Island Export Finance Ltd v Umunna* (1986), the court found in favour of the director. There are difficult judgements to be made between the duty not to exploit an opportunity on the one hand and the right of a director to take up opportunities after he or she has left the company on the other, and each case will be decided on its own facts.

8. There are a number of other instances that would fall within s 175, for example a director must not compete with his or her company (*Hivac v Park Royal* (1946)). Problems may also arise when a person holds directorships in competing companies: *Plus Group Ltd v Pyke* (2002) and see now also s 175(7).

9. It has long been recognised that a director may enter into a transaction in which he or she has a conflict of interest if he or she has the informed consent of shareholders in general meeting. In practice, articles of association often allow for disclosure to the board of directors instead. Under CA 2006, authorisation by the directors is now the default position in the case of a private company and in the case of a public company is sufficient if the constitution so provides (s 175(4) and (5)).

10. Authority of the board is effective only if the decision of the board is made independently of the director or directors in question (s 175(6)). Furthermore, the function of receiving disclosures cannot be delegated to a committee of the board (*Guinness plc v Saunders* (1990)).

11. The consequences of breach of the duty to avoid conflict of interest are:
   - a contract entered into in breach of the duty is voidable at the option of the company, subject to the rights of *bona fide* third parties, undue delays in rescinding the contract and affirmation of the contract by the company;
   - the director must account for any gains.

12.2.6 Duty not to accept benefits from third parties

1. Section 176(1) provides that a director of a company must not accept a benefit from a third party conferred by reason of his being a director or his doing (or not doing) anything as director.

2. The general duty set out in s 176 is an aspect of the no conflict principle. The section reformulates the principle of equity that a person in a fiduciary position must not accept a bribe. A benefit may take any form, financial or non-financial. However, s 176(4) provides that the duty is not infringed if acceptance of the benefit cannot reasonably be regarded as likely to give rise to a conflict of interest.

3. There is some overlap between ss 175 and 176, and some situations will fall within both. An important difference between the two sections is that s 176 does not provide for disclosure to and authorisation by the board of directors and it seems that the acceptance of benefits can only be authorised by the members.

12.2.7 Duty to declare an interest in a proposed transaction with the company

1. Under s 177 a director must declare to the other directors the nature and extent of any interest he may have in a proposed transaction or arrangement with the company, whether his interest is direct or indirect.

2. The section covers proposed transactions and disclosure must be made before the transaction is entered into by the company (s 177(4)). Declarations of interest in existing transactions or arrangements are covered by the provisions in ss 182–187.

3. The disclosure under s 177 may be made by written notice, general notice or statement at a meeting of directors (s 177(2)).

12.3 Other statutory provisions regarding directors' interests

Companies Act 2006 Part 10 Chapter 4	Transactions with directors requiring approval of members
s 188	Directors' service contracts where the guaranteed term of employment is or may be longer than two years
ss 190–196	Directors' contracts with the company where the director acquires a substantial non-cash asset from the company or where the company acquires a substantial non-cash asset from the director
ss 197–214	Loans to directors

12.3.1 Directors' service contracts

1. The consent of members is required if a director's service contract includes a guaranteed term of employment of more than two years (s 188 CA 2006).

2. Section 189 provides that if the requirements set out in s 188 are breached the service contract is deemed to contain a term allowing the company to terminate it at any time by reasonable notice.

12.3.2 Substantial property transactions

1. Contracts between directors and the company itself fall outside the scope of s 177 discussed above.

2. Under ss 190–196 contracts under which a director or a connected person acquires a substantial non-cash asset from a company or its holding company require the approval of members. The same applies if a company or holding company acquires a substantial non-cash asset from a director or connected person.

3. A substantial asset is defined as one which:
   - exceeds 10% of the company's asset value and is more than £5,000, or
   - exceeds £100,000.

4. Exceptions are set out in ss 192–194.

5. Section 195 provides that a contract made in contravention of these requirements may be avoided by the company, and the director or connected person is liable to account to the company for any gain and to indemnify the company for any loss or damage resulting from the transaction.

6. Under s 196 it is provided that if within a reasonable period a transaction which was not approved is affirmed by members it will no longer be voidable.

12.3.3 Loans to directors: ss 197–214

1. Previously loans to directors were prohibited (s 330 CA 1985). Now, under s 197(1) and (2) CA 2006 a company may not make a loan, give a guarantee or provide security in connection with a loan to a director or a director of its holding company unless the transaction has been approved by a resolution of members.

2. A memorandum setting out the nature of the transaction, the amount of the loan and the purpose for which it is required and the extent of the company's liability under the transaction must be made available to all members.

3. For public companies there are more extensive provisions relating to quasi-loans (defined in s 199), loans and quasi-loans to persons connected with directors (ss 198–200) and credit transactions (s 201).

4. Any transaction which contravenes these provisions (to which there are exceptions) is voidable at the instance of the company (s 213), unless:
   - restitution is no longer possible;
   - the company has been indemnified for any loss or damage resulting from the transaction;
   - rights acquired by a third party in good faith, for value and without actual notice of the contravention would be affected by the avoidance.

5. Under s 214 such breach can be affirmed by members.

12.3.4 Exemption from liability

1. Any attempt to exempt a director from liability for breach of duty by a provision in the articles or other document is void (s 232 CA 2006).

2. By virtue of s 234 a company can insure its directors against liability incurred to a person other than the company for breach of duty, but not for liability to pay a fine in criminal proceedings.

3. Section 235 provides for pension scheme indemnity whereby a director may be indemnified against liability incurred in connection with the company's activities as trustee of the scheme.

4. In an action involving breach of duty, a court may relieve a director of liability, in whole or in part, if the director has acted honestly and it appears to the court that he or she should be excused in the light of all the circumstances (s 1157 CA 2006): see for example *Re Duomatic Ltd* (1969).

13

Insider dealing and market abuse

Insider dealing – Part V Criminal Justice Act 1993

- S 52 CJA 1993 – the offence is committed by an individual who has information as an insider and deals in price affected securities as principle or agent, encourages another to do so or discloses information otherwise than in proper performance of duties
- Applies only to companies quoted on regulated markets
- Criminal penalties only
- Difficulties of prosecution and proof – enforcement ineffective

INSIDER DEALING AND MARKET ABUSE

Market abuse – Financial Services and Markets Act 2000 as amended

- S 118 FSMA defines forms of market abuse
- Enforced by Financial Services Authority
- Range of sanctions available, including provision for financial penalties for conduct that does not amount to a criminal offence
- S 119 FSMA 2000 – FSA must issue Code of Market Conduct

13.1 Introduction

1. Insider dealing is an offence under the Criminal Justice Act 1993 (CJA 1993). The offence may be committed by an individual who uses unpublished information about the company, acquired by virtue of his position, to deal in price sensitive securities so as to make a profit or avoid a loss.

2. In recent years such conduct has been seen as a breach of trust by a person in a fiduciary position and as a fraud on other investors. Since 1980, it has been a criminal offence. The law was revised in the Company Securities (Insider Dealing) Act 1985 and amended by the Financial Services Act 1986.

3. In 1989, an EC Directive (89/592/EEC) was adopted. This was designed to ensure that regulation of insider dealing was co-ordinated across member states and required that certain changes be made to the United Kingdom law. The law, now more focused on control of securities markets than on abuse of confidential information, is contained in the Criminal Justice Act 1993.

4. Some commentators argue against the criminalisation of insider dealing. Professor H.G. Manne in particular has put up a defence of the practice on the grounds that:
   - insider dealing should be seen as a legitimate benefit of management and a reward for entrepreneurial ability;
   - it is a 'victimless crime' since the fact that one party may have had inside information was irrelevant to the other party's decision to buy or sell;
   - it brings information to the market quickly;
   - it is notoriously difficult to prove and enforce and it is therefore futile to have the offence on the statute book.

5. These arguments have not been widely accepted and it is argued on the other hand that insider dealing:
   - involves an improper use of confidential information;
   - is contrary to the basic notion of market fairness as it places the insider at an unfair advantage.

   This view has prevailed in Europe.

6. However, there has been widespread criticism of the law as set out in the Criminal Justice Act 1993:
   - the Act provides for criminal penalties only;

- it applies only to companies quoted on regulated markets;
- prosecution under the Act has proved to be difficult and as a result there have been few prosecutions, so enforcement of the law has not been very effective.

7. The provisions introduced by the Financial Services and Markets Act 2000 (FSMA 2000) and strengthened by EC Directives, discussed at section 13.4 below, have sought to address some of these issues. The focus has moved in recent years from the criminal law of insider dealing to the regulation of market abuse and market manipulation under the FSMA 2000.

13.2 Insider dealing

13.2.1 The offence

1. The offence itself is set out in s 52 CJA 1993, and the terms used in s 52 are defined in ss 54–60. Section 53 provides for a range of defences.

2. Under s 52 an individual, who has information as an insider, may commit the offence in three ways:
   - s 52(1) dealing in price affected securities as principal or agent;
   - s 52(2)(a) encouraging another to do so;
   - s 52(2)(b) disclosing information otherwise than in the proper performance of his functions.

3. The offence extends only to regulated markets, or in circumstances where the person dealing relies on a professional intermediary or is himself a professional intermediary.

13.2.2 Definitions

1. Section 54 defines **securities** widely, to include certain options and futures as well as shares and debt securities.

2. Section 55(1) provides that a person **deals** if he or she:
   - acquires or disposes of the securities (whether as principal or agent), or
   - procures, directly or indirectly, an acquisition or disposal of the securities by any other person.

3. Under s 56, **inside information**:
   - relates to particular securities or to a particular issue of securities, not to securities generally;

- is specific or precise;
- has not been made public;
- would be likely to have a significant effect on the price of the securities if it were made public.

13.2.3 Who can commit the offence?

1. Under s 57 the offence can be committed only by an individual who has information as an insider.

2. An insider is defined as:
   - an individual who obtains information through being a director, employee or shareholder of the issuer of securities, or
   - an individual who has access to information by virtue of his employment, office or profession, whether or not his employment is with the issuer of securities, or
   - those who have inside information 'the direct or indirect source of which is a person falling into either of the first two categories'.

3. There is an exemption for market makers in relation to dealing or encouraging others to deal by s 53(4), as long as they act in good faith and in the normal course of business.

13.2.4 When is information made public?

1. Under s 58(2) information is made public if:
   - it is published in accordance with the rules of a regulated market for the purpose of informing investors and their professional advisers;
   - it is contained in records which are open to inspection by the public;
   - it can be readily acquired by those likely to deal in any securities to which the information relates, or of an issuer to which the information relates;
   - it is derived from information which has been made public.

2. Section 58(3) is also relevant and provides that information may be treated as made public even though:
   - it can only be acquired by persons exercising diligence or expertise;
   - it is communicated to a section of the public and not to the public at large;
   - it can be acquired only by observation;
   - it is communicated only on payment of a fee;
   - it is published only outside the United Kingdom.

13.2.5 Defences

1. Section 53 provides the following defences in relation to both dealing and encouraging:
   - that the defendant did not expect the dealing to result in a profit (or avoid a loss) attributable to the fact that the information was price sensitive;
   - that he or she reasonably believed that the information had been disclosed;
   - that he or she would have done what they did even if they had not had the information.

2. In relation to disclosing, the defences are:
   - that he or she did not expect any person to deal in the securities because of the disclosure;
   - that he or she did not expect the dealing to result in a profit attributable to the fact that the information was price sensitive.

13.2.6 Penalties

1. The offence is triable either way.

2. The maximum penalty on conviction on indictment is seven years imprisonment and/or a fine on which there is no limit, s 61(1). *R v Collier* (1987, unreported) is one of the few convictions leading to imprisonment.

3. Any transaction entered into in contravention of the act will stand – s 63, but will usually not be enforced by the courts (*Chase Manhatten v Goodman* (1990)).

13.2.7 Procedure

1. A prosecution can be instituted only by or with the consent of the Secretary of State for Business Innovation and Skills or the Director of Public Prosecutions (DPP). Suspected cases may be referred to the Department of Business Innovation and Skills from the Stock Exchange, which monitors the market.

2. The Financial Services Authority (FSA) may institute proceedings under s 402 FSMA (2000).

13.3 United Kingdom Listing Authority Model Code

1. Listed companies in the United Kingdom must have internal rules to govern dealings in securities by its directors, which must be at least as rigorous as the UKLA Model Code.

2. The Code lays down a number of principles to be followed by directors when dealing in their companies' securities, including the following:
   - A director of a listed company must notify the chairman (or another designated director) in advance of dealing in the company's securities. Dealings by the chairman or designated director must be notified to the board. A record of notifications and clearances must be kept.
   - A director of a listed company must not buy the company's securities during a 'close period', that is the two months before the preliminary announcements of its half-yearly and annual results or the month before the announcement of its quarterly results.

13.4 Market abuse

1. Since 1980 insider dealing has been a criminal offence in the United Kingdom. But it has been subject to criticism because of the difficulties in enforcing the law and the fact that it does not give rise to civil liability as well as criminal sanctions.

2. Directive 2003/6/EC (the Market Abuse Directive) applies to regulated markets in the EEA. The Financial Services and Markets Act 2000, as amended by the Directive, creates a statutory framework for the control of certain kinds of behaviour deemed to be unacceptable to the market, but falling short of criminal liability.

3. The purpose of the Directive is to:
   - preserve the integrity of financial markets, and
   - to enhance investor confidence.

   See *Spector Photo Group and Van Raemdonck v Commissie voor het Bank-, Financie- en Assurantiewezen* (2009) where the European Court of Justice (ECJ) was required to interpret the Directive in a case referred by the Brussels Court of Appeal.

4. The Act makes provision for financial penalties in cases involving market abuse, although this does not amount to a criminal offence.

5. As required by s 119 FSMA 2000, the Financial Services Authority has issued a detailed Code on Market Conduct.

13.4.1 What is market abuse?

1. Market abuse is defined in s 118 FSMA 2000, amended by SI 2005/381. Three forms of insider trading are defined as market abuse, along with six forms of market manipulation. The section describes conduct in relation to 'qualifying investments', which include company shares and debt securities, traded on a 'prescribed market'.

2. Insider trading as market abuse:
   - s 118(2) Insider dealing: where an insider deals, or attempts to deal, in a qualifying investment or related investment on the basis of inside information relating to the investment.
   - s 118(3) Improper disclosure: where an insider discloses inside information to another person otherwise than in the proper course of his employment, profession or duties.
   - s 118(4) Misuse of information: where the behaviour of a person is based on information not generally available and fails the regular user test; that is, the conduct would be regarded by a regular user of the market as a failure to observe the standard of behaviour of a person in that position.

3. Section 118B defines the term 'insider' as a person who has inside information:
   - as a director;
   - as a shareholder;
   - as a result of exercise of his employment, profession or duties;
   - as a result of criminal activities;
   - which was acquired by other means but he knows, or could reasonably be expected to know, that it is inside information.

4. Section 118C defines inside information in relation to qualifying investments as information of a precise nature which is:
   - not generally available;
   - relates, directly or indirectly, to issuers of the qualifying investments or to the qualifying investments;
   - would, if generally known, be likely to have a significant effect on the price of the qualifying investments or on the price of related investments.

5. Market manipulation as market abuse:
   (a) Effecting transactions which give, or are likely to give, a false or misleading impression as to the supply of, the demand for or price of qualifying investments (s 118(5)(a)).
   (b) Effecting transactions or orders to trade which secure the price of qualifying investments at an abnormal or artificial level (s 118(5)(b)). In the case of both (a) and (b) the behaviour is not market abuse if it is for a legitimate reason and in conformity with accepted market practices on the relevant market.
   (c) Effecting transactions or orders to trade which use fictitious devices or any other form of deception (s 118(6)).
   (d) Disseminating information which gives, or is likely to give, a false or misleading impression as to a qualifying investment by a person who knows or may reasonably be expected to know, that the information is false or misleading (s 118(7)).
   (e) Behaviour which is likely to give a regular user of the market a false or misleading impression as to the supply of, demand for or price of a qualifying investment which fails the regular user test (s 118(8)(a)).
   (f) Behaviour which would be, or be likely to be, regarded by a regular user of the market as behaviour that would distort, or would be likely to distort, the market in a qualifying investment and which fails the regular user test (s 118(8)(b)).

13.4.2 Enforcement

1. Enforcement of the market abuse provisions is the responsibility of the Financial Services Authority (FSA).

2. A range of sanctions is available to the FSA, from prosecuting through the courts for insider dealing (s 402 FSMA) to imposing its own sanctions, including a fine or a public reprimand.

3. The standard of proof is the civil standard (balance of probabilities) but this is subject to the principle that the more serious the allegation the stronger the proof must be: *Mohammed v Financial Services Authority* (FS&M Tribunal, 29 March 2005).

4. Under s 381 FSMA 2000 the FSA may apply to the High Court to issue an injunction restraining market abuse and, if satisfied that the person concerned was or may have been engaged in market abuse, a freezing injunction restraining the use of that person's assets may be issued by the court.

5. The FSA may make a restitution order against a person who has profited as a result of market abuse or where one or more people have suffered loss as a result. The FSA may also apply to the High Court for it to make an order.

14

Shareholder remedies

Derivative claims

The rule in *Foss v Harbottle* (1843)

Companies Act 2006, Part 11: The statutory derivative claim

s 260 – a member may bring a claim seeking relief on behalf of a company for a wrong done to a company

s 261 provides for a two-stage procedure

s 263(3) – factors the court must take into account in deciding whether to give permission for the claim to proceed

Personal claims by members

A member may initiate litigation to enforce a personal right enjoyed in the capacity of shareholder

Note the relevance of the statutory contract – s 33 CA 2006

SHAREHOLDER REMEDIES

Unfair prejudice

Sections 994–996 Companies Act 2006

Meaning of unfair prejudice
- must be unfair and prejudicial
- 'reasonable bystander'
- no requirement of intention or bad faith

The concept of 'legitimate expectation' was restrictively applied by the House of Lords in *O'Neill v Phillips* (1999)
Orders of the court – s 996
The most usual remedy is purchase of petitioner's shares

Just and equitable winding up

s 122(1)(g) IA 1986

Main reasons for use of remedy
- breakdown of trust and confidence in quasi-partnership
- deadlock
- lack of probity
- loss of substratum of company

14.1 Derivative claims

14.1.1 The rule in *Foss v Harbottle*

1. If a wrong is done to the company, the proper person to sue the wrongdoer is the company itself: this is the rule in *Foss v Harbottle* (1843).

2. There are three elements to the rule:
   - the proper claimant in an action in respect of a wrong alleged to be done to a company is the company itself;
   - the internal management principle: the courts will not generally interfere with matters of internal management of a company;
   - where the alleged wrong is a transaction which was done irregularly, but where the irregularity could be cured by a simple majority of the members, no individual member can bring an action in respect of that transaction (*MacDougal v Gardiner* (1875)). In such a case litigation would be futile.

3. Responsibility for decision-making in a company lies with either the board of directors or the shareholders in general meeting, by consent of the majority.

4. Difficulties may arise if the directors themselves are the wrongdoers since the right to litigate on behalf of the company is generally reserved to the board of directors (Art 3 of both the model articles for public companies and those for private companies limited by shares, *Breckland Group Holdings Ltd v London & Suffolk Property Holdings Ltd* (1989)).
   - To resolve this difficulty, the courts have exceptionally allowed an individual member to bring a derivative claim on behalf of the company.
   - A derivative claim is one where the right of action is derived from the company and is exercised on behalf of the company.
   - A derivative claim is an exception to the proper claimant principle. It arises only when proceedings are not instigated by the company in circumstances where a member or members consider a claim should be made and the court is willing to ignore the proper claimant principle.

5. In the course of the consultation process leading to the 2006 Act the Law Commission recorded a number of criticisms of the rule in *Foss v Harbottle* and the derivative claim: *Shareholder Remedies* (Law Com 246,

1997). It recommended partial abolition of the rule and a new derivative claim. This view was accepted by the Company Law Review. The *Final Report* recommended that derivative claims should be restricted to breaches of directors' duties and that they should be put on a statutory footing.

14.1.2 The derivative claim at common law

1. Prior to the Companies Act 2006, the courts were prepared to allow a derivative claim to proceed where minority shareholders were able to establish 'fraud on the minority' and that the wrongdoers were in control of the company.

2. The fraud on the minority exception was used sparingly as the courts were reluctant to hear cases brought against a director or other wrong-doer by an individual member on behalf of a company for a number of reasons:
   - the derivative claim undermines the concept of majority rule;
   - there is judicial reluctance to become involved in disputes over management and business policy;
   - the floodgates argument, that is, the fear that allowing these claims would result in a flood of actions by minority shareholders;
   - difficulties of proof, leading to protracted litigation;
   - the cost of proceedings and the question of who should pay. The company will benefit if the action succeeds, but does not want to undertake litigation (*Wallersteiner v Moir (No 2)* (1975)). In appropriate circumstances the courts will make a *Wallersteiner* order, ordering the company to fund the litigation.

3. A restrictive view of the scope of the derivative claim was taken, for example in *Prudential Assurance Ltd v Newman Industries* (1981) where it was held that there should be a preliminary action to establish that a *prima facie* case could be made, thereby extending the proceedings.

4. Other instances where claims have not been successful include:
   - where the court took the view that a majority within the minority of shareholders who were independent of the wrongdoers did not want to proceed with the claim: *Smith v Croft (No 2)* (1988);
   - where a more appropriate way of dealing with the matter was available: for example, *Cooke v Cooke* (1997), where the claimant had also petitioned under what is now s 994 CA 2006; *Mumbray v Lapper* (2005), where either of the parties could have sought relief either

by winding up on the just and equitable ground or under s 994 (see section 14.3 below);

■ where the claim was made for personal reasons rather than for the benefit of the company: *Barrett v Duckett* (1995);

■ where the claim was based on negligence on the part of the directors (*Pavlides v Jensen* 1956)), which can be contrasted with *Daniels v Daniels* (1978) where the claim succeeded because the negligence had resulted in the wrongdoers making a profit and was therefore deemed to be self-serving.

5. The Companies Act 2006 Part 11, Chapter 1 ss 260–264 now makes provision for a statutory derivative claim.

14.1.3 The statutory derivative claim

1. Part 11, Chapter 1 CA 2006 puts the derivative claim on a statutory footing and provides for a more flexible framework to allow a shareholder to pursue an action.

2. Under s 260 a shareholder may bring a claim seeking relief on behalf of the company for a wrong done to the company.

   ■ The claim may only be brought in respect of a cause of action arising from an actual or proposed act or omission involving negligence, default, breach of duty or breach of trust by a director, shadow director or former director of the company.

   ■ The claimant is not required to show wrongdoer control.

   ■ A claim may also be brought by an order of the court in proceedings under ss 994–996 (unfair prejudice).

3. Section 261 provides for a two-stage procedure:

   ■ the member must make a *prima facie* case to continue the derivative claim;

   ■ the court considers only the evidence presented by the claimant and if a *prima facie* case is not made the court will dismiss the case;

   ■ if the evidence supports a *prima facie* case the court may then give permission for the derivative claim to be heard.

4. Permission will be refused (s 263(2)) if the court is satisfied:

   ■ that a person acting in accordance with s 172 (duty to promote the success of the company) would not wish the claim to proceed;

   ■ in the case of an act or omission that is yet to occur, that the act or omission has been approved by the company;

   ■ in the case of an act or omission that has occurred, that the act or omission had been approved by the company beforehand or ratified afterwards: *Franbar Holdings v Patel* (2008).

5. Section 263(3) sets out the factors that the court must take into account in considering whether to grant permission to continue the claim. These include:

   (a) whether the member is acting in good faith;

   (b) the importance that a person acting in accordance with s 172 would attach to the claim;

   (c) where the act or omission is yet to occur, whether it is likely to be authorised or ratified by the company;

   (d) where the act or omission has occurred, whether it could be and is likely to be ratified by the company;

   (e) whether the company has decided not to pursue the action;

   (f) whether the act or omission in question gives rise to a claim that the member could pursue in his or her own right: see *Franbar Holdings Ltd v Patel* (2008).

6. Before the CA 2006 negligence alone, from which the director derived no personal benefit, was not sufficient to allow a derivative claim (*Pavlides v Jensen* (1956)). This restriction is not stated in s 260 and some commentators have expressed concern that this may result in large numbers of claims for negligence.

14.2 Personal claims

1. An individual shareholder may initiate litigation to enforce personal rights in relation to the internal management of the company. Such claims may arise in a number of situations.

2. Where a decision is taken that the company should enter into a contract that is outside the company's objects, a shareholder may bring an action to prevent the contract being concluded: *Simpson v Westminster Palace Hotel Co* (1860).

3. An action may be brought where the transaction requires a special majority but agreement has, for example, been achieved by an ordinary resolution: *Edwards v Halliwell* (1950).

4. Personal rights of a shareholder have been enforced where, for example:

   (a) dividends were paid in the form of bonds when the articles required payment in cash (*Wood v Odessa Waterworks Co* (1889));

(b) a member's vote was improperly rejected by the chairman of a general meeting (*Pender v Lushington* (1877));

(c) directors failed to allow a veto of a decision as provided in the articles (*Quin & Axtens Ltd v Salmon* (1909)).

In the context of the above examples, note the relevance of the statutory contract (s 33 CA 2006 discussed in chapter 4 above).

14.3 The 'no reflective loss' principle

1. In some circumstances, the loss suffered by the company may affect the shareholders or others, for example the share price may fall or the company may not be able to pay a dividend. The no reflective loss principle means that a member may not bring a personal action against the wrongdoer to recover a loss that just reflects the company's loss.

2. The principle ensures that a person can only be sued once for the damage caused and where the damage is caused to the company, the company is the proper claimant.

3. The principle applies even where:
   - the member has a personal cause of action against the defendant: *Day v Cook* (2001);
   - the company decides not to take action against the wrongdoer: *Johnson v Gore Wood & Co* (2003).

4. However, an exception to the rule exists where the failure to recover the loss is the fault of the wrongdoer. For example, in *Giles v Rhind* (2002) Rhind's wrongdoing had caused the company to go into liquidation. The company had started an action against Rhind but the administrator had been obliged to discontinue the claim for lack of funds. Giles, a shareholder, was able to claim.

14.4 Unfair prejudice

Section 994(1) CA 2006 provides that a member may petition the court 'on the ground that the company's affairs are being or have been conducted in a manner which is unfairly prejudicial to the interests of its members generally, or to some part of its members (including at least himself)'. This section (first enacted as s 75 CA 1980) replaced s 210 CA 1948 which provided a remedy for 'oppressive' conduct and had been very restrictively interpreted by the courts.

14.4.1 Who can petition?

1. A claim may be made by:
   - members of the company;
   - those to whom shares have been transferred by operation of law, for example personal representatives, trustees in bankruptcy.

2. A person may only petition as a member, but it is recognised that the interests of a member are not necessarily limited to constitutional rights. See for example *Re a company (No 00477 of 1986)* (1986). Furthermore, the 'interests of members' is not restricted to interests held in their capacity as members, as long as there is a sufficient connection with membership: *Gamlestaden Fastigheter AB v Baltic Partners Ltd* (2007). It should also be noted that 'interests' are wider than 'rights'.

3. There is no requirement of 'clean hands' (in contrast to the remedy under s 122(1)(g) Insolvency Act 1986: see section 14.5 below) but the conduct of the petitioner may affect the remedy (*Re London School of Electronics* (1986)) or the decision as to whether s 994 applies (*Woolwich v Milne* (2003)).

14.4.2 Meaning of 'unfairly prejudicial conduct'

1. Conduct must be both unfair and prejudicial (*Re BSB Holdings Ltd (No 2)* (1996)).

2. However, in contrast to the way the courts interpreted s 210 of the 1948 Act, the terms 'unfair' and 'prejudicial' have been given a very wide interpretation.

3. The courts have employed the concept of the reasonable bystander in determining unfair prejudice.

4. There is no need, in proving unfairness, to show either intention or bad faith (*Re RA Noble & Sons (Clothing) Ltd* (1983)). The test is whether it could be reasonably considered that the conduct unfairly prejudiced the petitioner's interests.

5. Prejudice does not necessarily require a reduction in the value of the petitioner's shareholding and may be shown in a number of ways:
   (a) Exclusion from management, if this breaks a mutual understanding about the management of the company: *Re a Company (No 00477 of 1986* (1986)); *Richards v Lundy* (2000)). However, this will not be

unfairly prejudicial if the directorship is unlawful, as in *Hawkes v Cuddy* (2007) where it was in breach of s 216 Insolvency Act 1986.

(b) Failure to pay dividends duly declared: *Re Sam Weller & Sons Ltd* (1990); failure by directors to even consider payment of a dividend to shareholders when they themselves were well remunerated: *Re McCarthy Surfacing Ltd* (2008).

(c) Payment of excessive remuneration to directors: *Re Cumana* (1986).

(d) Diversion of corporate assets, financial benefit or corporate opportunity (*Re London School of Electronics Ltd* (1986)); *Little Olympian Each-ways Ltd (No 3)* (1995).

(e) Packing the board with directors having interests adverse to the company (*Whyte, Petitioner* (1984)).

6. In general, mismanagement will not amount to unfair prejudice (*Re Elgindata Ltd* (1991)), but serious or gross mismanagement has been considered prejudicial (*Re Macro (Ipswich) Ltd* (1994)).

7. The section has been interpreted to include not only a breach of the company's constitution, but also a failure to meet the 'legitimate expectations' of a member or members. In the case of small private companies, the legitimate expectations may be outside of the constitution (*Re Saul D Harrison & Sons Ltd* (1994); *Richards v Lundy* (2000)). However, the courts have not been willing to recognise legitimate expectations beyond the constitution, as it appears in its public documents, in the case of public companies (*Re Blue Arrow plc* (1987); *Re Tottenham Hotspur plc* (1994)).

8. In *O'Neill v Phillips*, the House of Lords had the first opportunity to consider the unfair prejudice provisions, including the application of the concept of 'legitimate expectations' and held:
   - the phrase 'legitimate expectation' should be interpreted restrictively;
   - 'equitable considerations', which may be wider than the shareholder's strict constitutional rights, could be taken into account in appropriate circumstances.

9. In this case, although the petitioner might have had an expectation that his shareholding would be increased and the profit shared equally, the majority shareholder (Phillips) had made no unconditional promise to do this and it was therefore not unfairly prejudicial to the petitioner that it was not done.

14.4.3 The orders of the court

1. It is important to note the scope and flexibility of the orders available to the court. The court has freedom to make whatever order is deemed appropriate in the circumstances, but some specific orders are set out in s 996 CA 2006. These are:
   - to regulate the company's affairs in future (*Re Harmer Ltd* (1958), a case heard under the 'oppressive conduct' provision s 210 CA 1948);
   - to order the company to do or refrain from doing something;
   - to authorise civil proceedings to be brought in the name and on behalf of the company;
   - to require the company not to make alterations to its articles without the leave of the court;
   - to order the purchase of the petitioner's shares, at a price that reflects the value of the company.

2. The most common remedy is an order of the court for the purchase of the petitioner's shares. See *Grace v Biagiola* (2006) for a discussion of the remedy. The following principles are applied:
   - the shares are normally purchased at their full value and are not discounted to reflect the fact that they represent a minority holding;
   - the conduct of the petitioner (for example if he or she was in any way to blame for the breakdown) may be relevant and the shares may be discounted to reflect this;
   - usually the valuation will be calculated as at the time of the order, but the court has discretion in fixing the date and may fix it at the time of the petition;
   - if the parties cannot agree, the price should be set by an independent valuer.

14.4.4 The future of the remedy?

1. The introduction of the 'unfair prejudice' provisions now contained in s 994 CA 2006 has given minority shareholders an important remedy.

2. However, it has been criticised for the length and complexity of cases and the cost involved in bringing a case (*Re Unisoft Group Ltd (No 3)* (1994)) and for the fact that it may allow minority shareholders to enforce their will over that of the majority (*Re a Company (No 004377 of 1986)* (1986).

3. In *O'Neill v Phillips* (1999) the House of Lords reviewed the development of the law relating to unfair prejudice and clarified many

important aspects. The influence of the decision can be seen in recent cases, for example *Re GN Marshall Ltd* (2001); *Re Phoenix Office Supplies Ltd* (2003).

14.5 Winding up on the just and equitable ground

1. The Insolvency Act 1986 (IA 1986) provides a rather drastic remedy for a dissatisfied shareholder, used mainly in situations involving small closely-held companies (quasi-partnerships) where the relationship of trust and confidence has broken down.

2. Section 122(1)(g) provides that the company may be wound up if the court is of the opinion that it is just and equitable that the company should be wound up.

3. Section 124 IA 1986 provides that an application can be made by anyone who is a contributory. A contributory is a person who is liable to contribute to the assets of a company in the event of its being wound up. A fully paid-up member who is not liable to contribute has to show that he or she has a tangible interest in the winding up.

14.5.1 Restrictions on the remedy

1. It is an equitable procedure, and there is therefore the requirement for 'clean hands' on the part of the petitioner. This means that misconduct by the petitioner himself with result in the remedy being refused.

2. Section 125(2) IA 1986 provides that the court may not order a winding up if there is an alternative remedy available to the petitioners, for example an offer to purchase the petitioner's shares at a reasonable price, and they have been unreasonable in not accepting it (*Re a Company (No 002567 of 1982)* (1983)). However, there have been circumstances where the alternative remedy has not been appropriate and the application for winding up has succeeded (*Virdi v Abbey Leisure* (1990)).

14.5.2 Reasons for applications for just and equitable winding up

1. Successful petitions have been made on the following grounds:
   - in the case of a quasi-partnership, that the relationship of trust and confidence has broken down (*Re Yenidje Tobacco Co Ltd* (1916)). The breach must be sufficiently serious to justify the winding up;
   - where deadlock exists in the management of a company (*Ng Eng Hiam v Hg Kee Wei* (1964));
   - lack of probity (*Loch v John Blackwood Ltd* (1924)) but the fact that directors are negligent and inefficient is not sufficient to show lack of probity (*Five Minute Car Wash Service Ltd* (1966));
   - loss of substratum of company (*Re German Date Coffee Co* (1882)).

2. In *Ebrahimi v Westbourne Galleries* (1973) Lord Wilberforce laid down general guidelines in cases involving quasi-partnerships and a breakdown of trust. There must have been:
   - a breakdown of trust and confidence;
   - reasonable expectation on the part of the petitioner of taking part in the management of the company;
   - a restriction on the sale of shares so that the petitioner is 'locked into' the company.

14.5.3 Scope of the remedy

1. In some cases where unfair prejudice cannot be shown, the court has ordered a winding up (*Re RA Noble (Clothing) Ltd* (1983)).

2. But a petition was refused in *Re Guidezone Ltd* (2000) on the ground that the proposition that winding up on the just and equitable ground is wider than s 994 CA 2006 is inconsistent with *O'Neill v Phillips* (1999).

15

Takeovers and mergers

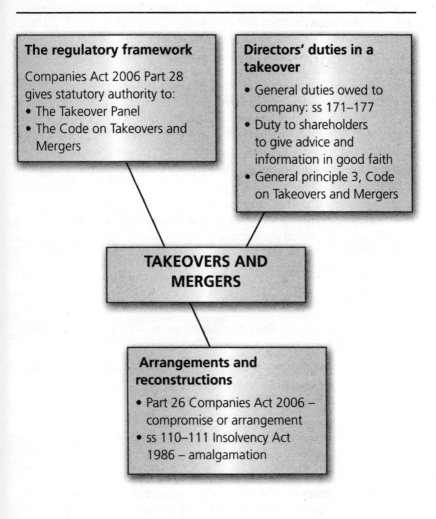

The regulatory framework

Companies Act 2006 Part 28 gives statutory authority to:
- The Takeover Panel
- The Code on Takeovers and Mergers

Directors' duties in a takeover

- General duties owed to company: ss 171–177
- Duty to shareholders to give advice and information in good faith
- General principle 3, Code on Takeovers and Mergers

TAKEOVERS AND MERGERS

Arrangements and reconstructions

- Part 26 Companies Act 2006 – compromise or arrangement
- ss 110–111 Insolvency Act 1986 – amalgamation

Part 28 of the Companies Act 2006, which deals with takeovers, gives statutory authority to the Takeover Panel and introduces a number of complex new provisions. The first part of the chapter focuses on the role of the Takeover Panel and the City Code on Takeovers and Mergers. Section 15.6 considers compromises and arrangements (Part 26 CA 2006) and reconstructions (ss 110–111 IA 1986).

15.1 Introduction

1. A takeover is usually understood to mean the process by which one company gains control of another.

2. This is usually achieved by the purchase by the offeror company of shares in the offeree company.

3. Rather than receiving payment in cash, shareholders, who must agree to the purchase, will frequently acquire shares in the offeror company.

4. In private companies a share sale agreement is usually made between the offeror company and shareholders in the offeree company.

5. Private companies often have a provision in the articles of association allowing directors to refuse to register a transfer of shares, so that a takeover will not be possible without the authority and consent of the directors.

6. Public companies can offer shares to the public and may be listed on the Stock Exchange. They often have large and dispersed shareholdings.

7. The usual procedure is for the offeror company to send a circular to the shareholders in the offeree (or target) company making an offer to buy their shares.

8. The directors of the offeree company must then take professional advice and make a recommendation to the shareholders whether or not they should accept the offer.

9. The terms 'merger' or 'acquisition' are often used where the undertaking, property and liabilities of two or more companies are transferred to another company. This may be one of the original companies or it may be a new company. All or substantially all of the shareholders of the original companies become shareholders in the new company.

15.2 Part 28 Companies Act 2006

15.2.1 Background

1. Following a number of scandals concerning takeovers and mergers, the Code on Takeovers and Mergers was published in 1967, and in 1968 a panel was established, made up of people with experience of the City and its institutions.

2. Until May 2006 the Takeover Panel had no statutory authority and no legal powers of enforcement. It was a self-regulatory body, responsible for the regulation of takeovers of public companies in the United Kingdom within the framework of the self-regulatory rules contained in the City Code on Takeovers and Mergers.

3. In May 2006 the Takeover Directive (Interim Implementation) Regulations 2006, SI 2006/1183 came into force. This implemented the Takeover Directive (2004/25/EC) which set minimum standards on the regulation of takeovers of companies whose shares are traded on a regulated market.

4. Under the Directive member states are required to designate an authority to supervise takeover bids in accordance with rules made under the Directive. While the designated authority may be a non-statutory body, it must be recognised by national law. The regulations provided a statutory foundation for the work of the Takeover Panel.

5. The Takeover Directive required implementation by 20 May 2006 and the Takeover Directive (Interim Implementation) Regulations was a 'stopgap' measure to comply with EU law until the relevant sections of the Companies Act 2006 (CA 2006) were brought into force. Part 28 of the Act, which implements the Directive, was brought into force on 6 April 2007 and the Regulations were repealed.

6. CA 2006 provides a statutory foundation for the work of the Takeover Panel, providing a legislative framework and bringing to an end a long period of self-regulation.

7. Section 942 of the CA 2006 provides that the functions of the Panel on Takeovers and Mergers are conferred under Part 28 Chapter 1 of the Act.

8. The Act gives the Panel authority to make rules to give effect to the Takeover Directive (s 943), to give rulings on interpretation, application or effect of the rules (s 945), to impose sanctions on a person who has

acted in breach of the rules or failed to comply with a direction (s 952).

9. Until 20 May 2006, the Code did not have the force of law but worked on the premise that 'those who seek to take advantage of the facilities of the securities markets in the UK should conduct themselves in matters relating to takeovers in accordance with best business standards and so according to the Code'.

10. Section 955 CA 2006 now provides that the Panel may seek enforcement by the courts.

11. Section 953 provides for a new offence of failing to comply with the Takeover Directive in respect of certain documents issued in the course of a takeover.

15.3 The Takeover Panel

15.3.1 Composition and functions of the Panel

1. The panel is composed of:
   - the Chairman and Deputy Chairman, appointed by the Bank of England;
   - members who are representatives of leading City institutions.
2. It has the following functions now conferred by virtue of Part 28 CA 2006:
   (a) Legislative – it drafts the provisions of the Code and makes amendments. This function is undertaken by the Code Committee.
   (b) Interpretive – it interprets the Code as required in relation to particular cases and circumstances.
   (c) Monitoring/investigative – it establishes whether there has been a breach of the Code.
   (d) Enforcement – it ensures compliance with the Code:
      - if a breach is suspected, the company concerned is invited to appear before the Panel Executive;
      - if it is shown that a breach has occurred the Panel may issue either a private or a public reprimand, or the company may be reported to another United Kingdom or overseas authority or professional body, for example the Stock Exchange or the Financial Services Authority, which may take disciplinary action;
      - the Panel can also publish a statement to the effect that the offender is someone who, in the opinion of the Hearing

Committee, is not likely to comply with the code, which may result in members of certain professional bodies being required not to act for that person in certain transactions;

- s 954 now provides that the Panel can order compensation to be paid in certain circumstances;
- s 955 provides that on application by the Panel, a court may make whatever order it thinks fit if it is satisfied that there is a reasonable likelihood that a rule will be contravened or that a person has contravened a rule or disclosure requirement;
- decisions of the Panel may be reviewed by the Hearings Committee: s 951;
- the consequences of failure to comply with the rules governing bid documentation now also include criminal liability: s 953.

15.3.2 Judicial Review

1. It has been held that the Panel is subject to judicial review (*R v Panel on Takeovers and Mergers, ex parte Datafin* (1987); *R v Panel on Takeovers and Mergers, ex parte Guinness plc* (1990)). This is not affected by Part 28 CA 2006.

2. The courts have recognised that the Panel is required to make decisions quickly and with authority and may give a ruling for future guidance rather than reverse a past decision.

15.4 The Code on Takeovers and Mergers

1. Following implementation of the Takeover Directive and CA 2006, the rules set out in the Code now have a statutory basis. The eighth edition of the Code was published on 20 May 2006 and was amended on 6 April 2007 to reflect its statutory status. It is a lengthy document, containing six General Principles and a number of detailed Rules.

2. The main objectives of the Code are:
   - to ensure fair and equal treatment of all shareholders in relation to takeovers;
   - to provide an orderly framework within which takeovers are conducted.

3. The Code is not concerned with:
   - the financial or commercial advantages or disadvantages of a takeover. These are matters for the company and its shareholders;

■ issues such as competition policy, which are the responsibility of government and are dealt with by separate legislation.

15.4.1 Principles underpinning the code

The general principles are statements of acceptable standards of commercial behaviour and reflect the principles set out in Art 3 of the Directive. They are:

1. All holders of the securities of an offeree company of the same class must be afforded equivalent treatment; moreover if a person acquires control of a company, the other holders of securities must be protected.

2. The holders of securities of an offeree company must have sufficient time and information to enable them to reach a properly informed decision on the bid; where it advises the holders of securities, the board of the offeree company must give its views on the effects of implementation of the bid on employment, conditions of employment and the locations of the company's places of business.

3. The board of an offeree company must act in the interests of the company as a whole and must not deny the holders of securities the opportunity to decide on the merits of the bid.

4. False markets must not be created in the securities of the offeree company, of the offeror company or of any company concerned by the bid in such a way that the rise or fall of the prices of the securities becomes artificial and the normal functioning of the markets is distorted.

5. An offeror must announce a bid only after ensuring that he or she can fulfil in full any cash consideration, if such is offered, and after taking all reasonable measures to secure the implementation of any other type of consideration.

6. An offeree company must not be hindered in the conduct of its affairs for longer than is reasonable by a bid for its securities.

15.5 Directors' duties in a takeover

1. Directors owe fiduciary duties to the company, not to individual shareholders, and must not use their powers for an improper purpose (s 171 CA 2006; *Hogg v Cramphorn* (1967)).

2. A takeover situation may lead to certain conflicts of interest and it has been held that directors owe a duty to shareholders to ensure that any

information and advice is given in good faith and is not misleading (*Dawson International plc v Coats Patons plc* (1988)).

3. In addition, note General Principle 3 (see section 15.4.1) which requires directors of the offeree company to act in the interests of the company as a whole.

15.6 Arrangements and reconstructions

15.6.1 Part 26 CA 2006

1. A compromise or arrangement may be made under the Companies Act, Part 26. This allows the rights of both creditors and members to be varied.

2. Under s 896(1) an application may be made to the court by the company or any member or creditor of the company, or, if the company is being wound up or in administration, by the liquidator or administrator. The court may order a meeting of members or class of member, creditors or class of creditor to consider the proposal.

3. Section 897 requires that statements containing certain specified information must be circulated to creditors or members entitled to attend.

4. An arrangement will be binding on all members, class of members, creditors or class of creditors, as the case may be, if:
   - it is agreed by a majority in number representing three-quarters in value of those present and voting in person or by proxy at the relevant meeting, and
   - the arrangement is sanctioned by the court.

15.6.2 Amalgamations under ss 110–111 Insolvency Act 1986

1. A company in voluntary liquidation can carry out a transfer of its assets in exchange for shares in another company (the transferee company). The shares are then distributed to members of the transferor company.

2. The arrangement must be sanctioned by a special resolution of the transferor company. This must be a separate resolution, but it may be given at the same meeting as the special resolution required to put the company into voluntary liquidation.

3. A member who did not vote for the special resolution may write to the liquidator within seven days of the resolution being passed requiring the liquidator either to abstain from carrying out the arrangement or to purchase the member's shares at a price determined by arbitration. If invoked, this process can undermine the completion of the arrangement.

16

Company failure and liquidation

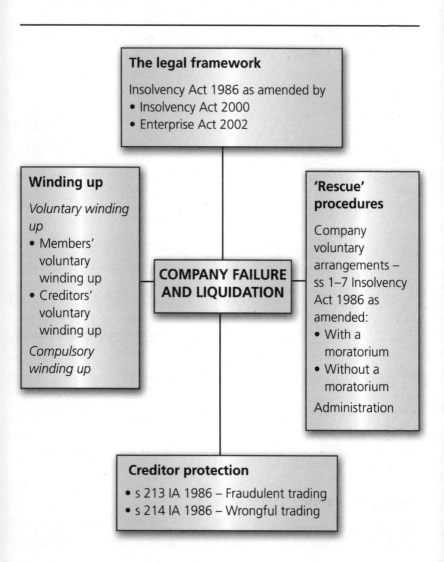

The legal framework

Insolvency Act 1986 as amended by
- Insolvency Act 2000
- Enterprise Act 2002

Winding up

Voluntary winding up
- Members' voluntary winding up
- Creditors' voluntary winding up

Compulsory winding up

COMPANY FAILURE AND LIQUIDATION

'Rescue' procedures

Company voluntary arrangements – ss 1–7 Insolvency Act 1986 as amended:
- With a moratorium
- Without a moratorium

Administration

Creditor protection
- s 213 IA 1986 – Fraudulent trading
- s 214 IA 1986 – Wrongful trading

16.1 The legal framework

1. The law governing insolvency and liquidation was changed and updated by the Insolvency Act 1985, following recommendations of the Cork Report, and is now contained in the Insolvency Act 1986 (IA 1986). Further changes have been introduced by the Insolvency Act 2000 and the Enterprise Act 2002.

2. The changes were intended to introduce procedures to facilitate the survival of a company in financial difficulty.

3. It is necessary to distinguish between insolvency procedures and liquidation procedures. Not all insolvency procedures result in the liquidation of the company and in some circumstances (notably the members' voluntary winding up and winding up on the just and equitable ground) a company that is not insolvent will be put into liquidation.

4. The law relating to insolvency and liquidation is complex and extensive and this chapter covers some general principles only.

16.1.1 Objectives of corporate insolvency law

The following objectives have been suggested:

1. To facilitate the recovery of companies in financial difficulty.

2. To suspend the pursuit of rights and remedies of individual creditors.

3. To prevent transfers and transactions which unfairly prejudice the general creditors.

4. To divest directors of their powers of management in certain circumstances.

5. To ensure an orderly distribution of the assets and a fair system for the ranking of claims.

6. To impose responsibility for culpable management by directors and officers.

16.1.2 Insolvency practitioners

All liquidation and insolvency procedures require the appointment of an insolvency practitioner to a particular office as shown in the chart below.

Procedure	Office
Administrative receivership	Administrative receiver
Administration order	Administrator
Voluntary arrangement	Supervisor
Liquidation (voluntary or compulsory)	Liquidator

16.1.3 Qualification

1. Only an individual can act as an insolvency practitioner, and he or she must not be:
   - an undischarged bankrupt;
   - subject to a director's disqualification order;
   - a patient within the meaning of the mental health legislation.

2. He or she must be qualified to act generally: recognised professional bodies can authorise persons to act as insolvency practitioners.

3. A person who acts without being qualified to do so commits a criminal offence.

16.2 Company voluntary arrangements

These are governed by ss 1–7 IA 1986 as amended by the Insolvency Act 2000. In its original form, a company voluntary arrangement (CVA) did not provide for a moratorium on payment of the company's debts, which meant that it was possible that a creditor would petition for a winding up before the CVA could be agreed. The amended legislation provides for two kinds of CVA: without a moratorium and with a moratorium, which allows the company time to come to a binding agreement with its creditors.

16.2.1 Company voluntary arrangements without a moratorium

1. A proposal is made for a composition in satisfaction of the company's debts or a scheme of arrangement.

2. The proposal may be made by:
   - the directors of the company, where the company is not in administration or in liquidation;
   - the administrator if the company is in administration;
   - the liquidator where the company is being wound up.

3. The role of the nominee:
   - a person who will supervise the implementation of the proposal, called the nominee, must be nominated;
   - a liquidator or administrator may act as nominee or may nominate another insolvency practitioner;
   - the nominee must submit a report to the court indicating whether he or she thinks the proposal should be put to meetings of creditors and members;
   - if the nominee thinks the proposal should be put to meetings he or she must call separate meetings of all creditors whose addresses are known and members.

4. The meetings may approve or modify the proposal, but cannot approve an arrangement which deprives a secured creditor of his right to enforce the security without the consent of the creditor. Nor can they approve a proposal which alters the priority of preferential debts.

5. Under s 4A IA 1986 (introduced by the Insolvency Act 2000) if the meetings come to different decisions the decision of the creditors must prevail. However, the members may apply to the court within 28 days and the court may order the decision of the members meeting to have effect or make any order that it thinks fit.

6. Once the proposal is approved, it binds all creditors who had notice and were entitled to vote at that meeting. However, there is a 28-day period within which application may be made to the court to have the proposal set aside.

7. Once approved, the arrangement is implemented by the nominee, who becomes the supervisor of the arrangement. When complete all creditors must be notified and must receive an account of receipts and payments.

16.2.2 Company voluntary arrangements with a moratorium

1. Company voluntary arrangements with a moratorium are governed by the Insolvency Act 1986 Schedule A1, introduced by the Enterprise Act

2002. The procedure may be used only by small companies as defined by s 382(3) of the Companies Act 2006 (CA 2006) and there are other restrictions on eligibility set out in Schedule A1.

2. The procedure is similar to that for a CVA without a moratorium except that:
   - the directors must apply for the moratorium;
   - they must give evidence that the company is likely to have sufficient funds to enable it to carry on business during the moratorium;
   - they must submit to the nominee any information he requires to enable him to form an opinion;
   - if the nominee forms a favourable opinion, the directors must file certain prescribed information with the court.

3. The effect of the moratorium is similar to an administration order, with the major difference that the directors retain their management role.

16.3 Administration

1. Unlike liquidation, which results in the company ceasing to do business, administration is designed to rescue the company, either as a whole or in part.

2. The law relating to administration orders has been overhauled by the Enterprise Act 2002 and is now contained in Schedule B1 of the Insolvency Act 1986 as amended. Previously only the court could appoint an administrator. An administrator may now be appointed by:
   - the court – application may be made by the company or its directors or by a creditor;
   - out of court appointment by the company or its directors;
   - out of court appointment by the holder of a qualifying floating charge.

3. The legislation provides for an hierarchical list of purposes. The administrator must perform his or her role with the objective of:
   - rescuing the company as a going concern, or
   - achieving a better result for the company's creditors as a whole than would be achieved if the company were wound up before going into administration, or
   - realising the property in order to make a distribution to one or more secured or preferential creditors.

4. The appointment of an administrator displaces the board of directors.

16.4 Receivers and administrative receivers

16.4.1 Appointment

1. A receiver is an individual appointed to take control of property which is security for a debt.

2. Receivers may be appointed by the court or in accordance with the terms of a debenture. Normally there is a clause in the charge which entitles the chargee to appoint a receiver.

3. An administrative receiver may be appointed by a creditor whose debt is secured by a floating charge on the whole, or substantially the whole, of the company's undertaking. He or she takes control of the whole, or substantially the whole, of the company's property. This right was abolished with respect to any floating charge created after 15 September 2003 by the Enterprise Act 2002. Holders of floating charges created before that date may still appoint an administrative receiver.

16.4.2 Effect of appointment of administrative receiver

1. The administrative receiver has sole authority to deal with charged property.

2. The directors continue in office but have no authority to deal with the charged property, so their role is extremely limited.

3. An administrative receiver is an agent of the company until the company goes into liquidation (IA 1986 s 44(1)(a)).

4. The administrative receiver must, within three months of appointment, prepare a report to be sent to the company's creditors and must call a meeting of unsecured creditors.

5. Apart from any contract for which specific performance may be ordered, the administrative receiver may cause the company to repudiate any existing contract.

16.5 Winding up

Winding up (liquidation) is the process whereby the company's assets are collected and realised, its debts paid and the net surplus distributed in accordance with the company's articles of association. Winding up is followed by dissolution of the company.

16.5.1 Voluntary winding up

The members adopt a resolution to wind up the company (special or extraordinary). This may result in a members' voluntary winding up or a creditors' voluntary winding up.

Members' voluntary winding up

1. The members of a company adopt a resolution to put the company into liquidation, following a statutory declaration by the directors that the company is able to pay its debts.

2. The members appoint a liquidator, usually at the meeting where the resolution to wind up the company is adopted.

3. On appointment of the liquidator, all powers of the directors cease.

Creditors' voluntary winding up

1. The members adopt a resolution to put the company into liquidation without a statutory declaration of solvency by the directors.

2. Members can nominate a liquidator, but the liquidator must hold a creditors' meeting at which they may nominate a liquidator, who will become the liquidator of the company unless the court directs otherwise.

3. The creditors may appoint a liquidation committee of up to five persons to act with the liquidator. Members may appoint five members to this committee.

16.5.2 Compulsory winding up

1. The court orders that the company be wound up on application to the court by a person entitled to petition. Section 124 provides that petitions may be made by:
   - any creditor who establishes a *prima facie* case;
   - contributories (shareholders who may contribute to the company's assets on liquidation);
   - the company itself;
   - the directors of the company;
   - a supervisor of a voluntary arrangement;
   - the clerk of the magistrates court if the company has failed to pay a fine;

- any or all of the parties listed above together or separately;
- the secretary of state;
- an official receiver – if the company is already in voluntary liquidation;
- an administrator of the company;
- an administrative receiver of the company.

2. The vast majority of petitions are by creditors.

3. The grounds on which a petition may be made are contained in s 122 Insolvency Act 1986. The most important are:
   - the company is unable to pay its debts (s 122(1)(f));
   - it is just and equitable to wind the company up (s 122(1)(g)).

16.5.3 Appointment and role of the liquidator

1. The official liquidator attached to the court where the order is made will be appointed.

2. If there are substantial assets, an insolvency practitioner may be appointed to replace the official liquidator.

3. Once the liquidator is appointed the directors cease to have any right to manage the company.

4. The role of the liquidator is to realise the assets and distribute them to those entitled to payment.

5. In an insolvent liquidation, priority of payment is important:
   (a) Where a debt is secured by a fixed charge, the asset charged may be taken in settlement of the debt. Charges secured by a floating charge are subject to the ring-fencing provisions of the Enterprise Act 2002 (see chapter 9, section 9.1.2 above).
   (b) The principle of set-off will allow a creditor who is owed money by the company to deduct the difference before paying the company, thus in effect receiving full payment of his debt to the company.

6. Subject to these two principles, the order of payment is:
   - expenses of the winding up, including the liquidator's remuneration;
   - preferential debts: up to four months' salary of employees, up to a prescribed amount, holiday pay and contributions to state and occupational pension schemes;
   - unsecured creditors;
   - deferred debts, for example debts due to a shareholder in his capacity as such, like dividends declared but not paid;

- where the company is not insolvent, any surplus will be distributed among members in accordance with class rights.

16.6 Fraudulent and wrongful trading

16.6.1 Fraudulent trading

1. Where a person (often, but not always, a director of a company) was involved in running a company which is in the course of being wound up and which was operated with the intention of defrauding creditors, the liquidator can apply to the court for an order that the person must contribute towards the assets of the company (s 213 Insolvency Act 1986).

2. In addition to civil liability, the director may be disqualified under the Company Directors Disqualification Act 1986 or prosecuted under s 993 CA 2006.

3. To establish fraud, intention or recklessness must be proved (*R v Grantham* (1984)).

16.6.2 Wrongful trading

1. A liquidator may apply for an order that a director, former director or shadow director of the company is liable to contribute to the company's assets if it can be shown that:
   - the company has gone into insolvent liquidation;
   - at some time before the start of the winding up, the director knew or ought to have known that there was no prospect of the company not going into insolvent liquidation; and
   - the director was a director at the time of the relevant transaction (s 214 Insolvency Act 1986).

2. The director's conduct should be judged against the standard of a reasonably diligent person having both:
   - the knowledge, skill and experience that would reasonably be expected of someone carrying out the same function, and
   - the knowledge, skill and experience of the director himself.

3. The main reason for these provisions is to compensate creditors in situations where directors have acted improperly in the ways described above. If the company is in insolvent liquidation cases are more likely

to be brought under s 214, where it is not necessary to prove fraud or dishonesty.

16.7 Dissolution

1. Dissolution of a company takes place when its name is removed from the register kept at Companies House. On liquidation, three months after the liquidator has sent his final accounts to the Registrar, dissolution automatically follows unless an application is made to the court seeking deferral of the date of dissolution. There are slightly different procedures for voluntary and compulsory liquidations.

2. There are a number of other ways in which dissolution may take place, including:

   - In an administration, three months after notification by the administrator that there is nothing to distribute to creditors the company is deemed to be dissolved.
   - By order of the court as part of a compromise, arrangement or reconstruction.
   - s 1000 CA 2006 sets out a procedure by which the Registrar is empowered to strike a company off the register. This accounts for a large number of dissolutions, where after sending letters to the company and advertising the Registrar is satisfied that the company has ceased to do business.
   - Under s 1003 CA 2006, on application of the company itself three months after publication of a notice in the Gazette.

Index